The RAIKES Bear & Doll STORY

by
Linda Mullins
Photography by **Linda Mullins**

Published by Hobby House Press™   Cumberland Maryland 21502

Additional Copies of this book may be purchased at $19.95
from
HOBBY HOUSE PRESS, INC.
900 Frederick Street
Cumberland, Maryland 21502
or from your favorite bookstore or dealer.
Please add $3.30 per copy postage.

Printed in the United States of America
ISBN: 0-87588-376-1

Table of Contents

Dedication

To Cathy and Robert Raikes Sr., Bob Raikes' wonderful parents.

Introduction

I feel very proud to author this book about Robert Raikes. Since the first time I met him in 1982, I have admired his values and philosophy of life, and his unbelievable talent as an artist and sculptor.

I hope his story of a struggling young artist who worked his way to become one of the most well-known and respected teddy bear artists of the 1980-1990s will inspire other talented artists striving to succeed.

Working in the wood-carving field for nearly two decades, the book reflects on the many hard times Raikes and his family experienced on the long road to success.

Beginning his career hand-carving wooden life-size birds, figures and mantels, Robert Raikes perfected a unique style of wood carving that he not only loved, but he found profitable — creating dolls and teddy bears.

His continued success earned him the recognition as a wood-carver and won him a cherished position in the collectors' world.

Robert Raikes has the gift of blending art and nature, enabling him to express unique personalities in his realistic animal creations.

Unable to meet the increasing demand for his original teddy bears and dolls, Robert Raikes now has a unique association with the well-known gift company, Applause, Inc., to reproduce his original creations. Together they continue to bring the collectors unequaled collectible designs.

Acknowledgements

I wish to thank the following people for making *The Raikes Bear & Doll Story* possible.

My sincere gratitude goes to Bob and Carol Raikes, for allowing me to write the inspiring story of their lives and career.

A special thank you to Cathy and Robert Raikes Sr., Bob's wonderful parents who opened up their home and their hearts to me by sharing personal stories of their son's life, allowing me to photograph their entire collection of his creations and hunting for days to find valuable photographic examples of their son's early work.

My sincerest appreciation to Peter and Janice Spitzer for sharing their extensive collection of Raikes products with me and their vast knowledge of his work.

To Elizabeth Wardley, Marketing Communications Manager at Applause, for her kind cooperation regarding Raikes Creations by Applause.

A great big thank you to my new friends, Robert and Pat Woodman, for supplying me with numerous photographs and information on Robert Raikes products by Applause.

To my very special friend Georgi Bohrod Rothe, my deepest appreciation for her encouragement and suggestions, and Editor Donna H. Felger for her invaluable advice and patience.

To my publisher, Gary Ruddell, for his support and his faith in me and this book.

Finally, no words can express the gratitude I have for the continued love and tolerance my husband, Wally, has given me.

Illustration 1. Robert Raikes at nine months old. Courtesy of Cathy and Robert Raikes Sr.

Chapter One

The Life of Robert Raikes

The Raikes bear story is of a young artist who conceived the idea of creating teddy bears with hand-carved wooden faces. Over the years, Robert Raikes worked his way to become one of the most famous teddy bear artists in the history of the craft.

Born on October 13, 1947, in Van Nuys, California, Bob Raikes was the oldest son among the three children of Robert and Cathy Raikes. As his father's work caused them to move about frequently, Bob traveled considerably as a child. The family even lived in England for a year.

Bob had no formal art education or training. He feels he inherited his talent of drawing from his father, who was a cartoonist. Bob recalls that the first carving he ever did was in junior high school, when he carved the face of his friend on a small piece of wood and presented it to her on a church camping trip. He does not remember carving again until 1969.

He was serving three years in the United States Navy and was stationed in southeast Asia. He carved the word "love" on a block of wood he found on the Navy base and mailed it to his teenage sweetheart, Carol, who was later to become his wife. This early representation of Bob's work is Carol's most cherished possession.

In 1970, when Bob was discharged from the service, he married Carol. In 1973, he enrolled as a student at the California Polytechnical College. During the summer break at the college, he met Gilbert Valencia, the chief carver for the Wetherby Rifle Company. Valencia was also noted for his religious carvings. Bob was fascinated by the elderly Mexican's carvings.

Valencia allowed Bob to watch him on a regular basis. "I think he thought I was only going to last a couple of days," Bob recalls. "But those days turned into months. After he saw that I was serious about carving, he let me use his tools, something he had never let anybody else do."

By the end of the summer, Bob had purchased his own tools and began to create his own style of carving. "I fumbled around with it for several years," he said of the wood sculpting.

As an enthusiastic artist, he joined the National Carvers Association and obtained a job teaching carving at Adult Education classes and local high schools. He began specializing in life-size birds and won an award for the best novice carver.

Bob loved what he was doing and after serious thought, he asked his wife, Carol, to keep her job as a dental assistant full-time for two years, allowing him to develop his new skills. His goal was to turn his hobby into a full-time profession. Bob worked 12 to 16 hours a day, carving everything from mantels and headboards, to figures and animals.

Illustration 2. Robert Raikes at eight years of age. Courtesy of Cathy and Robert Raikes Sr.

Illustration 5. On August 15, 1970, Robert Raikes married his teenage sweetheart, Carol. Courtesy of Cathy and Robert Raikes Sr.

Illustration 3. In 1956, Robert Raikes Sr. built this quarter Midget sports car for Bob to race at various race car events around the country. Courtesy of Cathy and Robert Raikes Sr.

Illustration 4. As a young boy, Bob became involved with 4-H, and proudly showed his steer (City Slicker) at the Antelope Valley Fair in Lancaster, California, in 1958. Courtesy of Cathy and Robert Raikes Sr.

Illustration 6. Bob and Carol Raikes with their young son, Jason. Courtesy of Cathy and Robert Raikes Sr.

In 1974, Bob's and Carol's first child, Jason, was born. One of the highlights of those early days was the sale of one of Bob's life-size eagles for $3500. In the little coastal town of Morro Bay, California, where the Raikes family lived for awhile, Bob was commissioned to carve a life-sized pelican, (*Illustration 10*) by Hofbrauer Restaurant, located on the Embarcadero.

I was thrilled to see this fine piece of workmanship when I visited Morro Bay in 1988. Morro Bay is now a popular resort town and Bob's pelican is enjoyed by thousands of tourists each year. Proudly standing with its wings lifted, ready for flight, it is a beautiful sight as it is silhouetted against the colorful sunsets. Examples of Bob's early work are visible all over the little beach town. Bob's attractive hand-carved wooden signs greeted my husband and me on the outside of many of the quaint shops (*Illustration 11*).

Then, one day in 1975, an admirer of Bob's work asked him to make some carved wooden dolls. "They turned out rather folksy-looking," said Bob. The heads were wood, with sawdust-filled cloth bodies (*Illustration 16*). But everyone appeared to like them. Since this was a new area for Bob, he was a little apprehensive to just concentrate on doll making. So, he kept carving his animals.

Bob asked Carol to continue working for another year, giving him one more year to try to make it as a carver. According to Bob, it was a do-or-die situation.

The cost of living was so high where the young couple lived that in 1978, they eagerly started a new life by purchasing five acres of their own land in the mountains of Grass Valley, California. Bob's dream was always to work among the trees and to breathe clean air. He felt this peaceful setting would allow him to really concentrate on his carving. With the help of Bob's father, they moved a trailer onto the property. As there was no electricity, they bought a generator, but most of the time used kerosene and propane.

"Life was pretty hard in the mountains at first for the kids," recalls Bob's father.

Their first major challenge was to dig a well. The ground was so rocky, Bob had to buy a hand-held well drilling outfit. There was a great deal of work to be done in these rugged mountains before the ambitious young couple could start their new life.

Bob still worked hard at his carving, cutting down his own trees and curing the lumber. He did well selling his carvings at craft shows and through his parents' antique shop in San Luis Obispo, California. But it seemed as hard as he worked, the young couple could not get ahead. Even the weather was against them. Their first winter in the mountains was the worst winter in Grass Valley in 30 years. The snow climbed above the windows of their little trailer. In 1978, when their second child, Jenny, was born, the couple decided the living conditions would be too hard on the new baby, so they left their beautiful mountains and moved back into town.

They moved frequently in the next few years in an attempt to outrun the spreading inflation. "We actually ran out of places to turn," Bob said. For extra money, he did odd jobs, yard work, picked apples, refinished furniture. Carol

Illustration 8. *Merlin. 1974. A Robert Raikes original. 11in (28cm) tall; sculptured in plastaline. Merlin was a practice piece for Robert Raikes that was never produced. The model was destroyed.* Courtesy of Cathy and Robert Raikes Sr.

Illustration 7. *Horse. 1972. A Robert Raikes original. 8in (20cm) long by 8in (20cm) tall; hand-carved oak driftwood; signed.*

One-of-a-kind. This was the "first" horse Robert Raikes carved from a piece of oak driftwood he found on the beach. Courtesy of Cathy and Robert Raikes Sr.

Illustration 9. *Eagle. 1974. A Robert Raikes original. 4.5ft (136cm) tall; all hand-carved wood; signed.*
One-of-a-kind. Carved from a solid black walnut stump. Courtesy of Cathy and Robert Raikes Sr.

Illustration 10. *Pelican. 1974. A Robert Raikes original, all hand-carved driftwood.*
Robert Raikes was commissioned to carve this life-size pelican by the Hofbrau Restaurant located on the waterfront at Morro Bay, California. This fine example of Bob's work is enjoyed by thousands of tourists each year. Proudly standing with his wings lifted, ready for flight, it is a beautiful sight as it is silhouetted against the colorful sunsets. Courtesy of Hofbrau Restaurant, Morro Bay, California.

Illustration 11. Robert Raikes' parents were proud to show me the early examples of their son's work that were visible all over the little beach town of Morro Bay, California. Bob's attractive hand-carved wooden signs greeted my husband and me on the outside of the quaint shops. During the artist's early years of carving, he was often given commercial commissions.

Illustration 12. Robert Raikes began hand-carving life-size birds early in his career. This magnificent and very difficult carving, Gulls in the Breeze, *was created from a large alder driftwood stump in 1975. Approximate size, 72in (213cm) tall. Courtesy of Robert and Carol Raikes.

Illustration 13. Carved Face. 1975. A Robert Raikes original. 14in (36cm) tall; all hand-carved wood.

One-of-a-kind. An ancient wooden mask was the inspiration for this fine example of Raikes' early carvings. Courtesy of Robert and Carol Raikes.

ABOVE: Illustration 14. Virgin of Guadalupe. *1976. A Robert Raikes original. 36in (91cm) tall; all hand-carved wood; signed. Robert Raikes carved this magnificent one-of-a-kind commissioned piece out of a willow stump.* Courtesy of Robert and Carol Raikes.

Illustration 15. Gnome. *1976. A Robert Raikes original. 8in (20cm) tall; all hand-carved wood; signed.*
One-of-a-kind. Seated gnome playing a wind instrument. Courtesy of Robert and Carol Raikes.

encouraged him all the way. Eventually, the couple decided to rent a home in Mount Shasta, California. As wood has always been Bob's focal point, he felt he would achieve his best work among the trees and mountains, an environment he found inspirational.

Between 1974 and 1976, Bob carved approximately a dozen miniature carousel horses (*Illustration 17*). In 1975, he formed two half-scale models (*Illustration 18*). However, it was Bob's grand life-size carousel horses that generated much attention during his earlier days. In 1981, he designed two magnificently carved carousel horses for the Holiday Inn in Santa Margarita, California. These gaily painted works of art were used as part of the inn's carousel (*Illustration 20*).

These early carousel horses sing with a tune all their own. The process for these colorful creatures takes a month. It begins with design work and after a full-scale sketch of the horse is finished, Raikes planes and glues the wood. The work must be perfect and can become quite tedious. A band saw cuts sections of wood and the pieces are glued together.

Then comes the sanding, by far the most time-consuming activity. Finally, Raikes constructs a "hollow box" for the body, carefully adding legs, head and tail with precision and care, one piece at a time. Once the body is completed, the horses are lacquered and painted.

When the finished work is over, Raikes faces the problem of shipping. Once, one horse arrived in Arizona with two broken legs. (The tail is removable so at least that appendage arrived intact.)

As more and more people requested his dolls, he decided to put all his efforts into just making dolls. Bob felt these were more lucrative and the new area was a challenge to him.

As always, Carol supported his efforts. She now worked right along Bob, making clothes and bodies for the dolls. Miraculously, things began to improve for the struggling young artist who, up until this time, had spent most of his married life just trying to pay the bills.

Illustration 16. *Girl Doll. Circa 1975. A Robert Raikes original. 27in (69cm) tall; hand-carved wooden head and shoulder plate; long red cotton yarn hair; sawdust-filled cloth body; hand-painted dark brown eyes and eyelashes; hand-carved signature and number on shoulder plate. Wearing a dark blue floral print dress and white pinafore.*

Example of one of the first dolls Robert Raikes created. This was entirely the artist's own impression of how a doll should look, as he had never been to a doll show or even known of their existence. Courtesy of Cathy and Robert Raikes Sr.

Illustration 17. *Miniature Carousel Animals. 1976. Robert Raikes originals. (Left) Standing lion. 5in (13cm) long by 4in (10cm) tall; hand-carved wood; hand-painted. (Center) Standing horse. 9in (23cm) long by 9in (23cm) tall; hand-carved wood; hand-painted. (Right) Jumping Horse. 4.5in (12cm) long by 4.5in (12cm) tall; hand-carved wood; hand-painted.*

The animals were mounted on metal poles and wooden bases. Each piece was different. Courtesy of Cathy and Robert Raikes Sr.

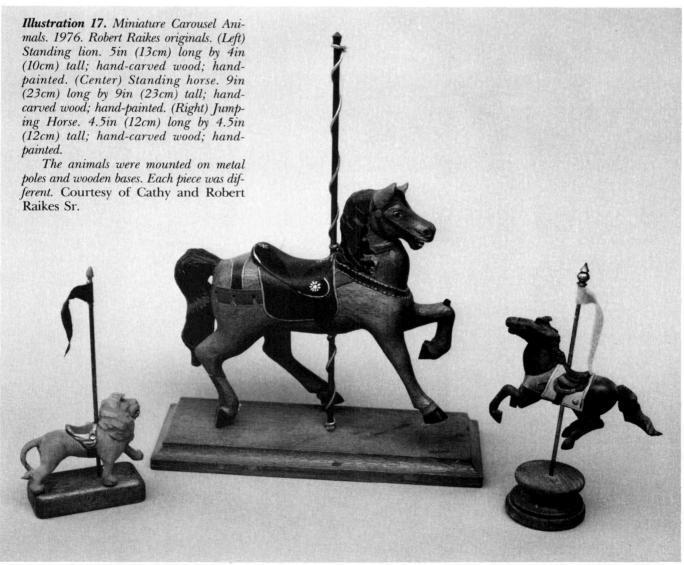

Illustration 18. *Carousel Horse. 1976. Robert Raikes original. 22in (56cm) long by 22in (56cm) tall; hand-carved redwood; hand-painted; 16 jewels.*

One-of-a-kind. Note the fine detail in the carving of the mane and saddle. Horse mounted on brass pole and metal base. Courtesy of Cathy and Robert Raikes Sr.

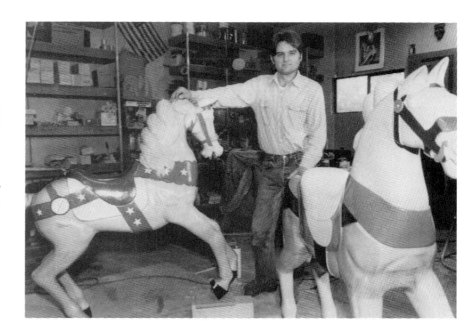

RIGHT: Illustration 20. *Life-size Carousel Horses. 1981. Robert Raikes originals; all hand-carved wood.*

Robert Raikes stands with two of his carousel horses that were destined for the Holiday Inn in Santa Margarita, California. These gaily painted works of art were part of the Inn's carousel. Courtesy of The Mount Shasta Herald.

BELOW: Illustration 19. *Robert Raikes Sr. proudly stands by one of his son's magnificently carved life-size carousel horses.* Courtesy of Pizazz Antiques, Morro Bay, California.

Illustration 21. Moroccan Drummer. *1977. A Robert Raikes original. 27in (69cm) tall; all hand-carved wood; signed.*
One-of-a-kind. Carved from a solid walnut log. Courtesy of Robert and Carol Raikes.

Illustration 22. Robert Raikes won the award for the best novice carver when he entered his life-size barn owl in the "Fly Away" contest in 1981. Raikes intricately hand-carved this realistic-looking bird in 1977. Courtesy of Robert and Carol Raikes.

Illustration 23. Ibis. 1979. A Robert Raikes original. 29in (74cm) tall; all hand-carved wood; hand-carved on left foot of bird on the right "Raikes."

This magnificent one-of-a-kind piece was carved from one piece of wood. Courtesy of Peter and Janice Spitzer.

Nervously, Bob and Carol Raikes exhibited at their first doll show in 1981. It was a small event in Santa Rosa, California, that really featured miniatures. Bob designed approximately 20 miniature dolls especially for the event. These were the only miniature dolls he remembers making. The apprehensive couple's fears were soon overcome by the response of the collectors at the show. By the end of the day, they were overwhelmed by their total doll sales of $800. Seeing the potential at the doll shows, they decided to exhibit at a major event in Anaheim, California.

The enthusiastic couple worked night and day and made a total of 32 dolls in three months. As the Anaheim show was a long distance for the couple to travel with their two small children, Bob's parents, who lived closer to the event, offered to work the show for them. As an added attraction, the senior Raikes created a miniature carousel, complete with music for the dolls to ride. Bob's father tells how the promoter of the show came by their booth and looked at the dolls as they were setting up and said, "I hope you have a lot of these dolls, as I have a feeling they won't last long."

Sure enough, even before the show opened, the dealers began to surround the table, buying like crazy. They were fascinated with the dolls' wooden faces, as this was quite revolutionary in the doll-making world. Mr. Robert Raikes Sr. recalls how he was forced to remove some of the dolls from the sales tables or he would have had no merchandise for the collectors when the show opened.

"The response from the public was even more overwhelming," Mr. Raikes Sr. said. "By the first half of the first day of the show, we sold all of the 32 dolls. We grossed $10,000. I couldn't wait to phone my son and tell him the wonderful news."

Bob remembers running through the house after his father phoned shouting, "Bingo! We've hit the right thing at last!"

For the next four years, Bob and Carol diligently worked to the early hours of the morning creating dolls. Bob carved. Carol sewed the bodies and the clothes. Bob's parents did their part, too. They agreed to work all the Southern California shows.

Around 1981, Bob began to see teddy bears enter into the doll scene and become quite popular. So, in 1982, he ventured into the teddy bear market. Mr.

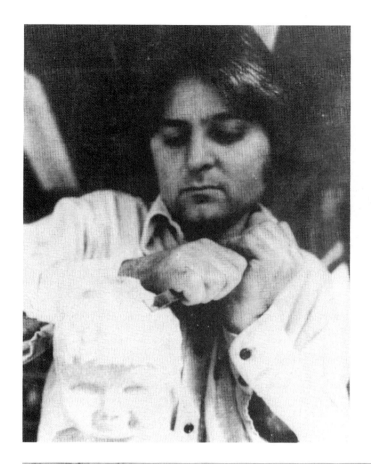

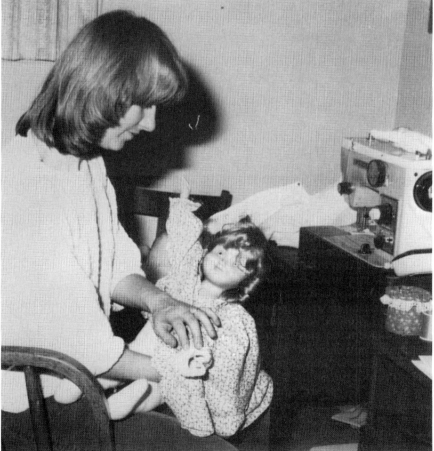

ABOVE LEFT: Illustration 24. *As more and more collectors requested Robert Raikes dolls, he decided to put all his efforts into just making dolls.* Courtesy of Mount Shasta Herald.

ABOVE RIGHT: Illustration 25. *Robert and Carol Raikes posed for this group portrait with a selection of their hand-carved wooden dolls for the* Mount Shasta Herald *in 1982.* Courtesy of Mount Shasta Herald.

LEFT: Illustration 26. *Working right along with her husband, Carol Raikes spent hours at her sewing machine creating the bodies and the outfits for the Raikes original dolls.* Courtesy of Mount Shasta Herald.

Raikes Sr. came up with a name for Bob's new creations; they were to be called *Woody Bears.*

When the bears were first introduced, Mr. Raikes Sr. recalls they did not receive quite the favorable response as the dolls. Their faces and feet were carved wood with jointed fur bodies that were stuffed very compactly and as a result, were quite heavy.

"The collector's first response was to touch their wooden faces," said Bob's father.

Cathy Raikes said, "I was surprised by the number of men that were fascinated by the bears and how they were made. They appeared to appreciate them as a form of art."

Each show the sale of bears increased. It was not long before the sales of bears equaled that of the dolls. Because of the increase in demand for their bears, Bob's brother, Mike, the wood shop teacher at Mount Shasta High School, assembled the joints and stuffed the bears, while his wife, Cindy, helped Carol make the bodies.

"I had so much work I didn't know what to do," Bob explained. "It's been a tremendous journey for us." He gives credit to his devoted wife, Carol, by stating, "I can't say enough about the support my wife has given me."

By 1984, Bob and Carol had reached a point in their career when, although they were at last successful and had become recognized artists making a fairly good income, they were literally exhausted from putting in extremely long hours. They reinvested the profits back into the business, but with traveling expenses, rising costs of material and general overhead, the business did not show enough profit to warrant the hours they were working.

When asked one time at a show if he sold wholesale, Bob replied, "It seems like our product has always been retail/wholesale. We would sell for what we thought was retail and people would buy it and resell it." He went on to say, "By being really fair in keeping our prices low, I found this really promoted my product in those early days."

Illustration 28. *Pouty Boy Doll. Circa 1981. A Robert Raikes original. Approximate size 21in (53cm) tall; hand-carved wooden head, shoulder plate, hair and hands; cloth body; hand-painted brown eyes and blonde hair; hand-signed and numbered (B-31). Dressed in blue denim trousers and waistcoat with checkered shirt.*

Early version of a Raikes pouty boy doll. Courtesy of Cathy and Robert Raikes Sr.

Illustration 27. *Jennifer Raikes at four years old cuddles one of her father's early creations.* Courtesy of Mount Shasta Herald.

ABOVE: Illustration 29. *(Left) Boy Doll. 1981. A Robert Raikes original. 21in (53cm) tall; hand-carved wooden head, hair, shoulder plate and hands; cloth body; hand-painted brown hair and brown eyes; hand-carved on shoulder plate "Raikes '81 #B5." Dressed in green wool pants, white shirt and knitted brown wool vest. (Right) Girl Doll. 1981. A Robert Raikes original 21in (53cm) tall; hand-carved wooden head, shoulder plate and hands; cloth body; hand-painted blue eyes; brown synthetic hair; hand-carved on shoulder plate "Raikes #5 '81." Dressed in pink, blue and white check dress; white pinafore.*

Not too much detail was given to the carving of the hands of these early dolls. Courtesy of Cathy and Robert Raikes Sr.

Illustration 30. *A group of hand-carved pieces by Robert Raikes.* Courtesy of Robert and Carol Raikes.

17

Illustration 31. *Around 1981, Robert Raikes began to see teddy bears enter into the doll scene and become quite popular. So in 1982, he ventured into the teddy bear market. These rare examples of Robert Raikes first designs of teddy bears have hand-carved applied wooden noses and less pronounced features. Also, the eyes on these early designs were not "inset." Approximately ten of this design were produced. (Left) Woody Bear. 1983. A Robert Raikes original. 22in (56cm) tall; gold acrylic fur; hand-carved wooden face and foot pads; applied hand-carved wooden nose; yellow plastic eyes; hand-painted features; jointed arms and legs; swivel head; hand-signed, dated and numbered on foot in black ink "Raikes '83 B.B.101." (Center) Woody Bear. 1983. A Robert Raikes original. 17in (43cm) tall; pale beige acrylic fur; hand-carved wooden face and foot pads; applied hand-carved wooden nose; yellow plastic eyes; hand-painted features; jointed arms and legs; swivel head; hand-signed, dated and numbered on foot in black ink "Raikes '83 M.B.101." (Right) Woody Bear. 1983. Robert Raikes original 21in (53cm) tall; gray variegated acrylic fur; hand-carved wooden face and foot pads; applied carved wooden nose; yellow plastic eyes; hand-painted features; jointed arms and legs; swivel head; hand-signed, dated and numbered on foot in black ink "Raikes '83 B.B.100." Courtesy of Cathy and Robert Raikes Sr.*

Illustration 33. *A grouping of Robert Raikes' personal collection of his original bears and animals. This picture was taken in the beautiful woods surrounding the artist's Mount Shasta home. Courtesy of Robert and Carol Raikes.*

RIGHT: Illustration 32. *Bob demonstrates the changes and improvements he has made on his bears over the years by holding one of his earliest versions (1982) on the right and one of his favorite bears (1985) on the left. Courtesy of Robert and Carol Raikes.*

The young couple decided to approach various toy companies. They proposed a plan whereby Bob would design the bears and dolls and the companies would manufacture them. When they arranged a meeting with a well-known gift company, Applause (renowned for their products such as Smurfs and Walt Disney characters), the representatives of the company appeared to like the dolls more than the bears. However, they decided to manufacture the bears first as they were easier to reproduce than the dolls.

So, in 1984, a contract was signed and Robert Raikes licensed Applause to produce his creations. (For more information on Applause, please refer to Chapter Three — Robert Raikes' Designs Find a Home With Applause). In addition to the royalties Bob and his wife received for the design of the Robert Raikes "Original Line" for Applause, they still produced special order bears under the name *Woody Bear*.

The Applause bears, designed by Robert Raikes, were an instant success. Applause sold out the first edition of 7500 in three weeks. When the bears reached the retail stores, the situation was very similar. Collectors frantically drove all over the country trying to find a store that had at least one Robert Raikes bear for sale.

As the second edition was not scheduled to be released for ten months, there was quite a period before there would be more Robert Raikes bears on the market. So the suspense and interest in his products grew immensely among the collectors. By the time the second edition was released to the stores, its popularity became even more incredible. Collectors had purchased the bears from the catalogs before they even arrived in the stores.

"It was amazing," Bob told me. "There has hardly ever been a time when there are a lot of my products on the market." And so it goes on, edition after edition.

It has been five years to date since the first Robert Raikes bears appeared on the market, but their popularity continues to grow. With each edition, more and more collectors are captured by their warmth and unique appeal.

Illustration 34. Unable to meet the increasing demand for his original teddy bears and dolls, Robert Raikes approached the well-known gift company Applause to produce his creations. In 1984, a contract was signed. This is an early grouping of the first edition of Raikes creations (including Jamie and Sherwood) reproduced by Applause in 1985. Note: In the early stages of production of the first edition, Hucklebear has Woody Bear embroidered on his pocket and Eric also has Woody Bear knitted into his scarf. The name was soon changed in both cases to Raikes Bears. In addition, Chelsea's outfit was slightly different at this time. (For more information on these bears, please refer to Illustration 171.) Courtesy of Robert and Carol Raikes.

Illustration 36. Boy Doll. Circa 1976. A Robert Raikes original. 27in (69cm) tall; hand-carved wooden head, shoulder plate and hair; sawdust-filled cloth body; hand-painted blue eyes; hand-signed, dated and numbered on shoulder plate. Dressed in blue denim suit and red and white checked shirt.

Robert Raikes felt his first dolls were rather primitive-looking with long heavy bodies. As not too many of this early representation of Raikes dolls were produced, they are quite sought-after by collectors today. Courtesy of Robert and Carol Raikes.

Chapter Two

How Raikes' Dolls and Bears Came To Be

Illustration 35. Girl Doll. Circa 1975. A Robert Raikes original. Approximate size 28in (71cm) tall; hand-carved wooden head and shoulder plate; sawdust-filled cloth body; hand-painted eyes and eyelashes; black cotton yarn hair; hand-signed, dated and numbered on shoulder plate. Dressed in white and yellow floral print dress with white pinafore and yellow and white gingham hat.

One of the earliest examples of Robert Raikes dolls. Note sculptured cloth hands, hand-painted eyelashes and cotton yarn hair. Courtesy of Robert and Carol Raikes.

The creative work of Robert Raikes is visible all over America and also in parts of Europe and the Orient. The response from the public is overwhelming. What is it about his work that has captivated thousands of people of all ages in all walks of life? His creations are unlike almost anything on the market. They have a gentle, unique appeal. The fact that they are carved in wood in a natural style makes people react to them as if they were alive.

For years Robert Raikes was consumed by the desire to be a carver. He found himself caught up with the decisions of creating pieces just for the sheer fun of it or concentrating on turning his avocation into a profitable business that could support his wife and growing young family. Fortunately for the ambitious young carver, he found success in a sphere of his work that he enjoyed and was also profitable — creating dolls and teddy bears.

Although Robert Raikes is renowned for his teddy bears, he first became well-known as an artist in the doll world.

In 1975, when Bob was first commissioned to carve several dolls, he had never been to a doll show or was even aware of the existence of such an event. His first attempts were purely his own concept of how a doll should look. These early designs had a lot of character and people responded to them. However, Bob felt they were rather primitive.

Today, these dolls are highly prized collector's items as only a few of them were ever made.

Characteristic of these first Raikes dolls were hand-carved wooden heads and shoulder plates, painted eyes and sawdust-filled cloth bodies with long arms and legs. The girls' hair was made of long cotton yarn (*Illustration 35*), whereas the boys' hair was sculptured (*Illustration 37*). Due to the weight of the bodies stuffed with sawdust, within a year this was changed to the lighter polyester fiberfill stuffing. Cloth hands were changed to hand-carved wood (*Illustration 39*). The wood on the lower part of the arm varied in length. In addition, attractive synthetic wigs replaced the girls' cotton yarn hair.

The first three to four years of doll making Bob spent developing several different size little girl dolls, along with a few boy dolls. His goal at this point was to develop his skills in this field and create his own design of artist dolls. From

Illustration 37. (Left) Girl Doll. 1978. A Robert Raikes original. 27in (69cm) tall; hand-carved wooden head and shoulder plate; sawdust-filled cloth body; hand-painted brown eyes; brown synthetic hair (replaced); carved on shoulder plate "#1 Raikes '78." Dressed in red and white dress.

Early version of Raikes' dolls. Long heavy cloth body. The doll originally came with cotton yarn hair.

(Right) Jason. Pouty-face Boy Doll. 1975. A Robert Raikes original. 27in (69cm) tall; hand-carved head, shoulder plate and hair; sawdust-filled cloth body; hand-painted brown eyes, blonde hair; hand-carved on shoulder plate "Jason #1 '75." Dressed in black velvet suit and white shirt.

Named after Bob's son, Jason. Experimenting with facial expressions, Raikes created a line of pouty-face dolls. The inspiration came for this expressive childlike little face from observing his young son, Jason. Courtesy of Robert and Carol Raikes.

Illustration 38. (Left) Girl Doll. 1977. A Robert Raikes original. 14in (36cm) tall; hand-carved wooden head and shoulder plate; cloth body; hand-painted blue eyes; brown synthetic hair; hand-carved on shoulder plate "RWR '77." Dressed in blue, pink and white floral dress with matching hat.

(Right) Girl Doll. 1978. A Robert Raikes original. 15in (38cm) tall; hand-carved wooden head and shoulder plate; cloth body; hand-painted brown eyes; brown synthetic hair; hand-carved on shoulder plate "Raikes '78." Dressed in dark blue floral print dress.

Examples of Robert Raikes' early dolls. Note primitive carved features compared to his later work. Courtesy of Robert and Cathy Raikes Sr.

Illustration 39. *Pouty-face Boy Doll. 1980. A Robert Raikes original. 22in (56cm) tall; hand-carved wooden head, hair, shoulder plate and hands; cloth body; hand-painted blonde hair and blue eyes; hand-carved on shoulder plate "B2 Raikes 1980." Dressed in Levi overalls and red knitted sweater.*
    Wonderful hand-carved pouty-face. Note early primitive carved hands with no separation between fingers, sculptured tears on cheek. Courtesy of Nancy Page.

Illustration 40. *Gnome. 1980. A Robert Raikes original. 9in (23cm) tall; all hand-carved wood; hand-painted features; articulated head and body; separate hand-carved pipe and cane; clothes made of wool and dyed burlap. Hand-carved on back "Raikes."*
    One of the earliest dressed characters created by Robert Raikes. Courtesy of Robert and Carol Raikes.

Illustration 41. *Girl Doll. Circa 1981. A Robert Raikes original. Approximate size 17in (43cm) tall; hand-carved wooden head; shoulder plate; hands, lower legs and shoes; cloth body; hand-painted brown eyes; black synthetic hair; hand-signed, dated and numbered (SG27). Dressed in white and dark blue printed dress with white apron.*
    Early version of Raikes small cloth-bodied girl dolls. Note carved wooden shoes. Courtesy of Robert and Cathy Raikes Sr.

Illustration 44. A hang-tag "Hand Carved and Crafted Dolls by Bob and Carol Raikes" was attached to each doll. The tags for the dolls varied somewhat over the years. Courtesy of Robert and Cathy Raikes Sr.

Illustration 42. Boy Doll. Circa 1981. A Robert Raikes original. Approximate size 17in (43cm) tall; hand-carved wooden head, shoulder plate, hair, hands, lower legs and shoes; cloth body; hand-painted hair and eyes; hand-signed, dated and numbered. Dressed in black suit, white shirt and checkered hat.

The smaller size in the Raikes cloth bodied dolls were very slender with daintily carved features. Not too much detail was given to the carving of the hands and shoes of these early dolls. Courtesy of Robert and Cathy Raikes Sr.

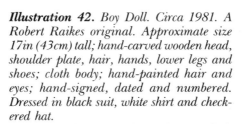

Illustration 45. A "Raikes Originals" certificate of authenticity for the dolls. This certificate accompanied each doll produced by Robert Raikes. The name and number of that particular doll, the date it was made was hand-written on each certificate. The design of the certificate changed over the years but the information remained the same. Courtesy of Robert and Carol Raikes.

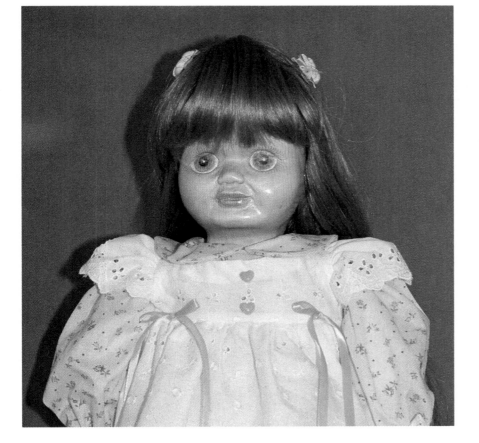

Illustration 43. Jenny. Girl Doll. 1981. A Robert Raikes original. 25in (64cm) tall; hand-carved wooden head, shoulder plate and hands; cloth body; "big" blue painted eyes; light brown synthetic hair; hand-carved on shoulder plate "Raikes '81 #G6." Dressed in blue print dress with a white pinafore.

Robert Raikes named this doll after his eldest daughter, Jenny. One of the "big-eyed" series of dolls. Courtesy of Robert and Pat Woodman. Photograph by Robert Woodman.

RIGHT: *Illustration 46.* Three examples of Robert Raikes' original basic doll designs showing the progression of his work.

(Right) First design. Girl Doll. 1978. Hand-carved wooden head and shoulder plate; hand-painted features; cloth body; long arms and legs; heavy sawdust-filled body; replaced synthetic wig (original wig was made of cotton yarn — Illustration 16).

(Center) Second design. Boy Doll. 1981. Hand-carved wooden head, hair, shoulder plate and hands; cloth polyester-filled body; hand-painted features.

Note the changes from the first design. The hands are now hand-carved wood. The body is changed to the lighter polyester stuffing. The limbs are in more proportion to the body and not so long. The head is affixed to the body in a neater, more professional manner. The bodies on the girl dolls were also changed to this design. In addition, the girls' hair was changed from cotton yarn (Illustration 35) to synthetic hair (Illustration 43).

(Left) Third design. Girl Doll. 1985. All hand-carved wood, articulated head and body; hand-painted features; synthetic hair.

In 1982, Robert Raikes began experimenting with carved wooden bodies with what he called "sophisticated joints." By 1987, the bodies of all Raikes dolls were completely carved of wood and jointed. Cloth-bodied dolls were only made by special order. Courtesy of Robert and Cathy Raikes Sr.

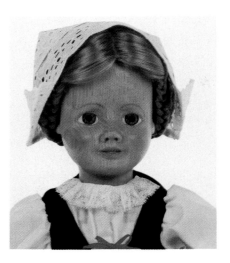

ABOVE: *Illustration 48.* Girl Doll. Circa 1981. A Robert Raikes original. 24in (61cm) tall; hand-carved wooden head, shoulder plate and hands; cloth body; hand-painted blue eyes; hand-signed, dated and numbered. Dressed in an Austrian-style outfit.

Note how artistic-looking Raikes dolls have become since his first attempt in 1975 (Illustration 35). Courtesy of Robert and Carol Raikes.

Illustration 49. Clown Doll. 1982. A Robert Raikes original. 22in (56cm) tall; hand-carved wooden head, shoulder plate and hands; cloth body; hand-painted eyes and clown face; yellow cotton yarn hair; hand-carved on shoulder plate "Raikes '82 #20." Dressed in red check with white collar clown suit.

Clown is seated on a metal tricycle made by Robert Raikes Sr. Courtesy of Cathy and Robert Raikes Sr.

Illustration 47. Girl Doll. Circa 1981. A Robert Raikes original. 24in (61cm) tall; hand-carved wooden head, shoulder plate and hands; cloth body; brown synthetic hair; hand-painted "big" brown eyes; hand-signed, dated and numbered. Dressed in a pink and blue dress.

Exploring the limits of expression, Robert Raikes produced a small series of dolls with big painted eyes. They are referred to as the Raikes "big-eyed" series. Note that more detail is now given to the hands. Courtesy of Robert and Carol Raikes.

LEFT: Illustration 51. Jester *Doll. Circa 1982. A Robert Raikes original. 18in (46cm) tall; hand-carved wooden head, shoulder plate and hands; cloth body; hand-painted eyes and face; red cotton yarn hair; hand-signed, dated and numbered. Dressed in a white, red and blue satin clown outfit.* Courtesy of Robert and Carol Raikes.

ABOVE: Illustration 50. Clown *Doll. 1982. A Robert Raikes original. 24in (61cm) tall; hand-carved wooden head, shoulder plate and hands; cloth body; hand-painted eyes and face; orange synthetic curly hair; hand-carved on shoulder plate "Raikes '82 #14B." Dressed in multi-colored striped clown outfit.*

The clown holds hand-carved wooden juggling balls. The large shoes were made by Robert Raikes' father. Courtesy of Robert and Pat Woodman. Photograph by Robert Woodman.

Illustration 52. Clown *Doll. Circa 1982. A Robert Raikes original. 22in (56cm) tall; hand-carved wooden head, shoulder plate and hands; cloth body; hand-painted blue eyes and clown face; sections of gathered red material for hair; hand-carved on shoulder plate "Raikes G327." Dressed in bright orange and red floral clown suit.* Courtesy of Debby Gong. Photograph by Roy H. Floyd.

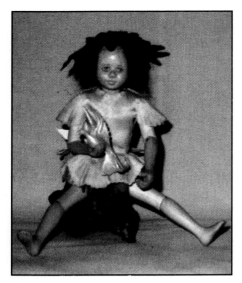

Illustration 54. Faerie *Doll. 1983. A Robert Raikes original. Approximate size 9in (23cm) tall; all hand-carved wood; articulated head and body; hand-painted blue eyes; synthetic brown hair; hand-signed and dated.*

First all hand-carved wooden Faerie *doll Robert Raikes created. Courtesy of Robert and Carol Raikes.*

the beginning, Bob was interested in making each doll look different, with its own character. He sincerely felt that each collector deserved something that was truly unique.

Experimenting with facial expressions early in his doll-making career, Bob began creating a line of pouty-face dolls. The inspiration came for this expressive childlike little face from observing his young son, Jason (*Illustration 37*).

After attending doll shows, Bob was fascinated by the soft beauty of the faces of the bisque antique dolls. Exhibiting at shows also put Bob in close contact with the collectors. Inspired by the antique dolls and conversing with the collectors, the enthusiastic young sculptor went on to create his series of "Little Wooden Children."

Each new doll produced was more sophisticated and intriguing than the last. The utmost detail was applied to the features. The bodies became much lighter and shapelier. A metal armature encased within the stuffing of the arms of the cloth-bodied dolls was designed to enable the arms to be posed or to hold a toy. Approximately 600 Raikes dolls were made with cloth bodies, the majority being sizes 24in (61cm), 14in (36cm) and a few smaller.

In 1982, Bob began experimenting with carved wooden bodies, with what he called "sophisticated joints." With his past experience in carving all-wood human sculptures, Bob found this type of body a natural and easy transition. However, the hard part was to accomplish the jointing method.

By 1987, the bodies of all Raikes dolls were completely carved of wood and jointed (*Illustration 64*). Cloth bodies were only made by special order.

Now these graceful elegant dolls could be posed.

Bob prided himself that no two dolls were alike. The many different expressions and varieties of dolls this talented artist created brought accolades from all corners.

Illustration 53. *(Left)* Peter. Boy *Doll. 1982. A Robert Raikes original. 23in (58cm) tall; hand-carved wooden head, shoulder plate, hair and hands; cloth body; hand-painted blue eyes and blonde hair; hand-carved on shoulder plate "Raikes '82 B28." Dressed in black velvet pants, variegated brown knitted vest, white shirt and brown and white wool hat.*
(Right) Shanna. Girl *Doll. 1982. A Robert Raikes original. 22in (56cm) tall; hand-carved face, shoulder plate and hands; cloth body; hand-painted brown eyes; blonde synthetic hair; hand-carved on shoulder plate "Raikes '82 G114." Dressed in gray and white print dress; white pinafore.*

A metal armature is encased within the stuffing of the arms of both dolls to allow the arms to be posed or hold a toy. Courtesy of Peter and Janice Spitzer.

Illustration 56. Jensine. *Black Girl Doll. 1983. A Robert Raikes original. 23in (58cm) tall; hand-carved wooden head, shoulder plate and hands; cloth body; hand-painted brown eyes; black synthetic hair; hand-carved on shoulder plate "Raikes '83 G275."* Dressed in pink print dress with white cotton pinafore.

Robert Raikes made very few versions of a black doll. Courtesy of Peter and Janice Spitzer.

Illustration 55. *A selection of Robert Raikes original hand-carved wooden doll heads, waiting to be assembled onto the cloth bodies. Note the wonderful variety of facial expressions. In some cases, before Bob made the bodies for the dolls, he would carve several different doll heads with different expressions and mail them to the collectors to choose the face they preferred.* Courtesy of Robert and Carol Raikes.

Illustration 57. *Black Boy Doll. 1983. A Robert Raikes original. 22in (56cm) tall; hand-carved wooden head, hair, shoulder plate and hands; cloth body; hand-painted black hair, brown eyes; hand-carved on shoulder plate "B89 Raikes '83."* Dressed in black velvet suit and white shirt.

Robert Raikes produced a very limited number of black boy dolls. Courtesy of Cathy and Robert Raikes Sr.

RIGHT: Illustration 60. Jester *Doll. 1984. A Robert Raikes original. Approximately 18in (46cm) tall; all hand-carved wood; articulated head and body; hand-painted eyes and face; brown feathers for hair; hand-signed and dated. Dressed in dark purple satin costume.* Courtesy of Robert and Carol Raikes.

FAR RIGHT: Illustration 58. Witch *Doll. 1983. A Robert Raikes original. 16in (41cm) tall; hand-carved wooden head; shoulder plate and hands; cloth body; black synthetic hair; hand-painted eyes; hand-signed and dated. Dressed in a black dress and cape.*

One-of-a-kind. Note the intricately carved features. Robert Raikes created the Witch *to exhibit at a doll show. She originally held a carved wooden apple with a worm crawling out of it.* Courtesy of Robert and Carol Raikes.

Illustration 59. Medieval Jester. *1984. A Robert Raikes original. 23in (58cm) tall; all hand-carved wood; articulated head and body; hand-painted eyes and face; black synthetic hair; hand-signed and dated. Dressed as a jester.*

Magnificent example of the exquisite workmanship of Robert Raikes' later work. Note unusual wrist joints. Courtesy of Robert and Carol Raikes.

Illustration 61. *Girl Doll. 1984. A Robert Raikes original. Approximately 26in (66cm) tall; all hand-carved wood; articulated head and body; hand-painted brown eyes; brown synthetic hair; hand-signed and dated. Dressed in blue and white dress.*

As each individual all hand-carved wood doll was so unique and not part of an edition, they were not numbered, only hand-signed and dated. Courtesy of Robert and Carol Raikes.

Illustration 63. Gretal. *Girl Doll. 1984. A Robert Raikes original. Approximately 26in (66cm) tall; all hand-carved wood; articulated head and body; hand-painted blue eyes; blonde synthetic hair; hand-signed and dated. Dressed in a German-style costume.*

Note how the hands and features have even more detail with each doll Raikes creates. Courtesy of Robert and Carol Raikes.

Illustration 62. *Girl Doll. 1984. A Robert Raikes original. Approximately 26in (66cm) tall; all hand-carved wood; articulated head and body; hand-painted blue eyes; black synthetic hair; hand-signed and dated. Dressed in a long rose pink and white print dress. Courtesy of Robert and Carol Raikes.*

Illustration 64. Gretal. *Girl Doll. 1984. A Robert Raikes original. 26in (66cm) tall; all hand-carved wood; articulated head and body. Undressed version of* Illustration 63 *showing the workmanship of Raikes all hand-carved wood doll body. Courtesy of Robert and Carol Raikes.*

Illustration 65. Faerie Doll. 1984. A Robert Raikes original. Approximately 12in (31cm) tall; all hand-carved wood; articulated head and body; hand-painted eyes; synthetic brown hair; hand-signed and dated. Dressed in dark green tulle skirt with silk flowers and feather accessories.

Raikes, always into his imagination, gives life to Faeries. Produced between 1983 to 1986, the majority stand about 12in (31cm) tall. Approximately eight were made, as their very delicate features were extremely difficult to produce. Courtesy of Robert and Carol Raikes.

Illustration 66. Faerie Doll. 1984. A Robert Raikes original. 12in (31cm) tall; all hand-carved wood; articulated head and body; hand-painted blue eyes; synthetic brown hair; hand-signed and dated. Dressed in dark lavender silk skirt and top in the shape of flower petals.

Approximately eight Raikes Faerie dolls were produced between 1983 and 1986. Courtesy of Robert and Carol Raikes.

Illustration 68. Molly. Girl Doll. 1985. A Robert Raikes original. 16in (41cm) tall; all hand-carved wood; articulated head and body; hand-painted blue eyes; black synthetic hair; hand-written on shoulder plate in black ink "Raikes '85 #4." Dressed in pink dress.

Robert Raikes originally created Molly as a Christmas present for his mother. It was one of Bob's favorite dolls. He later made approximately three versions of this cute little girl doll. Reproduced by The Good Company in 1989 (Illustration 206). Courtesy of Robert and Carol Raikes.

Illustration 67. Baby Doll. 1985. A Robert Raikes original. 21in (53cm) tall; hand-carved wooden head, hair, shoulder plate and hands; cloth body; hand-painted blonde hair and blue eyes; hand-signed. Dressed in an early christening dress and bonnet.

One-of-a-kind. Created for Robert Raikes' mother. Reproduced by The Good Company in 1989 (Illustration 206). Courtesy of Cathy and Robert Raikes Sr.

Illustration 69. Little Red Riding Hood. 1984. A Robert Raikes original. 25in (64cm) tall; all hand-carved wood; articulated head and body; hand-painted eyes; brown synthetic hair; hand-signed and dated. Dressed in blue and white check skirt, blue and white print blouse and red cape. Courtesy of Peter and Janice Spitzer.

Bob hand-carved or hand-signed in ink his signature on the back of the all-wooden dolls and on the back of the shoulder plate of the dolls with cloth bodies. They were also dated and came with a certificate of authenticity.

The cloth-bodied dolls were numbered. For example, "G237" would be a girl doll #237. "B310" would be a boy doll #310. "SG28" would be small girl #28 and "SB39" would be small boy #39.

Because the all-wood dolls were so unique from each other and not part of editions, these dolls were not numbered. From the 800 dolls the imaginative artist produced, approximately 250 were not numbered. Also, as the dolls became more sophisticated, Bob decided to change the name of the "Little Wooden Children" to "Raikes Originals" (approximately 1982).

The dolls at that time were the family's entire source of income. The business was on the level of a cottage industry, being conducted out of the Raikes' home. Everyone became involved in their construction and sale.

The Raikes' home and workshop were filled with dolls in various stages of production. The children were continually surrounded by dolls to cuddle and play with. Bob describes what his house was like in those early doll-making days.

"A doll-making studio was a hectic environment in which to raise a family," Bob recalls. "There was a carving shop, a material storage room and an assembly sewing room. This sometimes overflowed into the living room, even though we tried to avoid it in order to keep an orderly house for the family. This was not always easy to do."

It took Bob and Carol approximately two days to make the small dolls and two or three weeks for some of the larger or more complicated ones. They worked 12 to 16 hour days.

Carol Raikes took care of the bookkeeping and also made numerous different outfits for all the dolls. It was also Carol's job to find a name that suited each doll. Carol said, "I looked through books and encyclopedias for hours looking for that perfect name."

It was the Raikes' children, Jason, Jenny and Emily's responsibility to give the dolls their final inspection before they were packed to go to the show.

By exhibiting their son's work at numerous doll shows, Bob's parents, Robert Raikes Sr. and his wife, Cathy, played an active and very supportive part in their son's career. Robert Raikes Sr. kept a record of every person that purchased Bob's early dolls from him. He would tell the collectors, "Someday my son will be really famous, and he may wish to contact you regarding events

OPPOSITE PAGE: Illustration 70. Little Red Riding Hood. *1983. A Robert Raikes original. 26in (66cm) tall; all hand-carved wood; articulated head and body; hand-painted brown eyes; blonde synthetic hair. Dressed in a blue and white dress with red cape.*
Wolf *Doll. 1983. A Robert Raikes original. 30in (76cm) tall; hand-carved wood head, shoulder plate, legs and paws; cloth body; hand-painted features; hand-signed in gold ink on shoulder plate "Robert Raikes 1983." Dressed in a gray check wool suit with white and gray striped shirt and red scarf.*

Wolf *sits on original hand-carved wooden tree stump. Hand-signed in gold ink on stump "Robert Raikes 1983." Note the fine detail in the carved mouth and tongue. Robert Raikes created two different versions of* Little Red Riding Hood and the Wolf. *Courtesy of Debby Gong.*

Illustration 71. Victorian Lady *Doll. 1985. A Robert Raikes original. 23in (58cm) tall; all hand-carved wood; articulated head and body; hand-painted brown eyes; brown synthetic hair; hand-written on back of doll "Raikes '85." Dressed in an elegant violet-colored silk skirt, cape and white blouse.*

Robert Raikes made approximately 25 elegant ladies. Because the all hand-carved wooden dolls were individually unique from each other and not part of an edition, these dolls were not numbered. Courtesy of Robert and Carol Raikes.

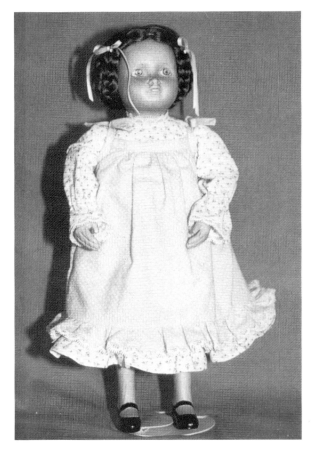

Illustration 72. Fawn Doll. 1986. A Robert Raikes original. 20in (50cm) tall; all hand-carved wood; articulated head and body; hand-painted brown eyes; synthetic light brown hair; hand-signed and dated.

One-of-a-kind. Note jointed wrists, carved hooves and teeth. Courtesy of Robert and Carol Raikes.

Illustration 75. (*Left*) Janice. *Girl Doll. 1985. A Robert Raikes original. 26in (66cm) tall; all hand-carved wood; articulated head and body; hand-painted brown eyes; synthetic blonde hair; hand-written in brown ink "Robert Raikes 1985." Dressed in pink and white stripe dress, blue apron and scarf.*

Note smiling face and carved teeth.
(*Center*) Jordan. *Girl Doll. 1984. A Robert Raikes original. 23in (58cm) tall; hand-carved wooden head, shoulder plate and hands; cloth body; hand-painted brown eyes; synthetic brown hair; hand-written on shoulder plate in brown ink "Raikes G84 '82." Dressed in cream and blue-colored polka dot dress trimmed with lace.*

(*Right*) Cheryl. *Girl Doll. 1982. A Robert Raikes original. 23.5in (58cm) tall; hand-carved wooden head, shoulder plate and hands; cloth body; hand-painted blue eyes; blonde synthetic hair; hand-written on shoulder plate in brown ink "G102 Raikes '82." Dressed in gray and white print dress with lace trim.*

Jordan *and* Cheryl *both have wire armature encased within the stuffing of the arms to allow the arms to be posed or hold a toy.* Courtesy of Peter and Janice Spitzer.

LEFT: Illustration 76. Pioneer Lady *Doll. 1985. A Robert Raikes original. Approximately 18in (46cm) tall; all hand-carved wood; articulated head and body; hand-painted brown eyes; brown synthetic hair; hand-signed. Dressed in blue and black dress with matching hat and white apron.*

Robert Raikes produced four versions of the Pioneer Lady *in different outfits.* Courtesy of Robert and Carol Raikes.

RIGHT: Illustration 77. Boy Doll. 1985. *A Robert Raikes original. Approximate size 21in (53cm) tall; hand-carved wooden head, shoulder plate, hair and hands; cloth body; hand-painted hair and eyes; hand-signed, dated and numbered. Dressed in short wool trousers and cap, white shirt and knitted vest.*

Robert Raikes' boy dolls are considered highly collectible as only a small percentage of the dolls he produced were boys. Courtesy of Robert and Carol Raikes.

BELOW: *Illustration 78.* Winter Lady *Doll. 1986. A Robert Raikes original. Approximately 18in (46cm) tall; all hand-carved wood; articulated head and body; hand-painted eyes; black synthetic hair; hand-signed and dated. Dressed in brown silk skirt, cape and hat and white blouse, carrying fur muff.* Courtesy of Robert and Carol Raikes.

Illustration 79. Oriental Lady *Doll. 1986. A Robert Raikes original. 22in (56cm) tall; all hand-carved wood including hair; articulated head and body; hand-painted brown eyes; black hair; hand-written on back "Raikes 1986." Dressed in maroon and white silk kimono (six layers of silk in kimono).*

Only two Raikes' Oriental Ladies were made. One doll had synthetic hair and one had hand-carved, black painted hair. Courtesy of Peter and Janice Spitzer.

Illustration 80. Faerie *Doll. 1986. A Robert Raikes original. 12in (31cm) tall; all hand-carved wood; articulated head and body; hand-painted brown eyes; synthetic brown hair; hand-signed and dated. Dressed in green tulle skirt with silk flowers.*

Note very delicate carved features. Courtesy of Robert and Carol Raikes.

that may interest you about his work." Sure enough, Bob's father's words came true and his conscientious work paid off. Approximately the first 1000 people that were contacted regarding the Robert Raikes Collector's Club, formed in June 1988, were names the proud father had so faithfully saved for all these years.

Looking back at those shows, Bob's father describes what Bob's dolls remind him of. "When the dolls were displayed at the shows, they reminded me of a group of school children as each one was so different."

Raikes has an uncanny ability to bring fantasy to a tangible state. For instance, his children and animal dolls are the sort that demand to be picked up and played with. Although they are fully jointed, posable and wear beautifully made removable outfits, it is their facial expressions which beckon the viewer. The animal dolls each have distinct personalities and seem like characters from childhood bedtime stories. Carol Raikes dressed these fantasy creatures with perfection and skill.

Raikes, always into his imagination, also gives life to fairies. Produced between 1983 and 1986, they stand approximately 1ft (31cm) tall and are all that your dreams could conjure up. Approximately eight were made, as their very delicate features were extremely hard to produce (*Illustration 66*).

As the dolls were individually hand-carved, Bob never knew as he was carving what their final expression would really be until the work was completed. He let the doll take on its own character. He knew what the basic look would be (e.g., smiling or pouty). "The face has to evoke emotion or a sense of wonder from those viewing the dolls on my end. I have to feel the work has challenged my creativity. In some cases, before I made the body for the doll, I would carve several doll heads with different expressions and mail them to the collectors to choose the face they preferred," Bob explained (*Illustration 55*).

When I asked the enterprising artist if he would name the various dolls he made, the year and the amount produced, he replied, "Linda, too much time has passed, and I have designed too many different items to be able to remember exact dates and numbers. I was always so busy trying to keep up with all the orders. At the time, I never realized the importance of keeping such records."

However, he talked enthusiastically of the dolls he could recall. "My favorite dolls are those dealing with fantasy and elegant ladies. It gives me a chance to daydream in art form. The elegant ladies were all-wood except for three. There were approximately 25 produced. Each was different. Several were exquisitely dressed in beautiful silk clothes. I made two Oriental ladies between 1985 and 1986. Each of these had six layers of silk in their beautiful kimonos (*Illustration 79*).

Illustration 82. Woody Bear. *1982. A Robert Raikes original. 7in (18cm) tall; beige acrylic fur; hand-carved wooden face; applied hand-carved nose; hand-painted features; unjointed body.*

This is the "first" teddy bear Robert Raikes ever made. It was a Christmas present for his mother. Note the small carved features and painted eyes. The nose was hand-carved separately and glued to the snout. Courtesy of Cathy and Robert Raikes Sr.

Illustration 81. The "first" attempt Robert Raikes made to create a bear's face was in 1982. Note how he originally tried wooden ears, an applied tiny carved nose and hand-painted eyes. This rare and interesting example of Raikes first bear's head would not have been saved had it not been for Robert Raikes Sr., who retrieved it from the trash where his son had discarded it the day before. At this writing, this design has never been reproduced. Courtesy of Cathy and Robert Raikes Sr.

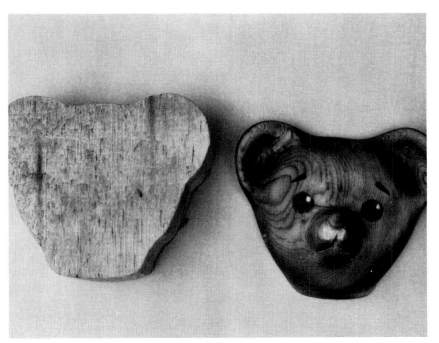

BELOW: Illustration 85. *An example of the identification marks on the first designs of Robert Raikes' Woody Bears. Hand-written in black ink, the letters indicate the size of the bear, for example, T. B. (Tiny Bear), S. B. (Small Bear), M. B. (Medium Bear), B. B. (Big Bear). This early identification method was soon changed with the introduction of the entire face of the bear carved from one piece of wood (Illustration 89). It appears on these first designs, the numbers (example, #101) did not specify the amount produced.* Courtesy of Cathy and Robert Raikes Sr.

Illustration 83. Woody Bear *(Prototype). 1982. A Robert Raikes original. 22in (56cm) tall; variegated beige acrylic fur; hand-carved wooden face; applied hand-carved wooden nose; hand-painted features; jointed arms and legs; swivel head.*

This is an example of one of the earliest designs of Raikes' teddy bears. It was an experimental piece, not made for resale. Note the applied separate hand-carved nose, painted eyes and acrylic fur paw and foot pads. Courtesy of Robert and Carol Raikes.

Illustration 84. *(Left)* Woody Bear. *1983. A Robert Raikes original. 17in (43cm) tall; pale beige acrylic fur; hand-carved wooden face and foot pads; applied hand-carved wooden nose; yellow plastic eyes; jointed arms and legs; swivel head; hand-signed and numbered on foot in black ink "Raikes 83 MB101." (Right)* Woody Bear. *1983. A Robert Raikes original. 22in (56cm) tall; gold acrylic fur; hand-carved wooden face and foot pads; applied hand-carved wooden nose; yellow plastic eyes; jointed arms and legs; swivel head; hand-signed and numbered on foot in black ink "Raikes '83. B. B. 101."*

Examples of the first bears Robert Raikes produced for resale. Note the flat face, shorter snout and small applied hand-carved wooden nose. In addition, the eyes on these early bears were not "inset." Also note the hang-tags are the same as used for the dolls. The Woody Bear tags were not yet in use. Approximately ten of this design were made. Raikes then created a more professional and appealing-looking bear with a longer pronounced snout and the face and nose which were all carved from one piece of wood, and the eyes were "inset" (Illustration 89). Courtesy of Cathy and Robert Raikes Sr.

Illustration 86. Woody Bears. 1983. Robert Raikes originals. 7in (18cm) tall; acrylic fur; hand-carved wooden snout; applied carved wooden nose; plastic eyes; unjointed body.

Examples of one of the experimental designs when Raikes first ventured into the teddy bear world. Approximately four were made. They were never produced for resale. Courtesy of Cathy and Robert Raikes Sr.

Illustration 87. Baby Woody Bear. 1983. A Robert Raikes original. 9in (23cm) tall; short beige acrylic fur; hand-carved wooden snout; brown Ultrasuede foot and paw pads; plastic eyes; red felt tongue; jointed arms and legs; swivel head; cry box encased in stomach.

Approximately two of this design of Raikes' baby bears were produced when Bob was first experimenting with different styles of hand-carved wooden faces. Courtesy and Cathy and Robert Raikes Sr.

Illustration 88. Woody Bear (Prototype). 1983. A Robert Raikes original. 22in (56cm) tall; beige acrylic fur; hand-carved wooden face and foot pads; brown plastic eyes; jointed arms and legs; swivel head.

Here we see basically the same early design as the bears in Illustration 84, but now the artist improves his technique for the nose by skillfully carving the face, snout and nose from one piece of wood. Note the eyes are changed to brown but are still not "inset." Note also the dark shading of the wood which was obtained by burning the wood, an early procedure that was later replaced by allowing the natural grain of the wood to show through. This experimental bear demonstrates the transition between the bear with the applied hand-carved nose (Illustration 84) to the more professional-looking bear with the face, snout and nose carved from one piece of wood (Illustration 89).

39

Illustration 89. Woody Bear. *1983. A Robert Raikes original. 21in (53cm) tall; pale beige acrylic fur; hand-carved wooden face and foot pads (early burnt wood method used); "inset" plastic eyes; jointed arms and legs; swivel head; "hard-stuffed body;" hand-carved on foot "Raikes '83 L025."*

An example of one of the earliest designs of bears produced for resale with the face, snout and nose hand-carved from one piece of wood. Note the characteristic of Robert Raikes' Woody Bears quickly progressed from the crude applied wooden nose to this far more professional-looking bear with the face, nose and snout all hand-carved from one piece of wood. In addition, the eyes are now skillfully inset into the wood. Note also the introduction of the firmer, more sculptured body, also the signature and identification marks are now hand-carved into the wooden foot pads. The tie was an addition to some of the early designs. Courtesy of Peter and Janice Spitzer.

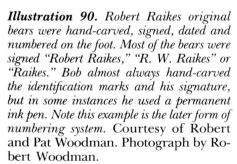

Illustration 90. *Robert Raikes original bears were hand-carved, signed, dated and numbered on the foot. Most of the bears were signed "Robert Raikes," "R. W. Raikes" or "Raikes." Bob almost always hand-carved the identification marks and his signature, but in some instances he used a permanent ink pen. Note this example is the later form of numbering system.* Courtesy of Robert and Pat Woodman. Photograph by Robert Woodman.

Illustration 91. Woody Bear. *1983. A Robert Raikes original. 24in (61cm) tall; long variegated beige acrylic fur; hand-carved wooden face and foot pads; inset plastic eyes; jointed arms and legs; swivel head; hard-stuffed body; signed, dated and numbered on foot.*

A wonderful example of an early bear with the burned wood effect. To obtain the look Bob wanted, he burned the wood with a blowtorch. He later accomplished this realistic effect by allowing the natural grain of the wood to show through. This bear was adopted by a collector at Linda Mullins' first San Diego Teddy Bear and Antique Toy Show and Sale in 1983. Courtesy of Robert and Carol Raikes.

LEFT: **Illustration 93.** Jamie (Prototype). Woody Bear. 1984. A Robert Raikes original. 10in (23cm) tall; short gray acrylic fur; hand-carved wooden face and foot pads; inset plastic eyes; jointed arms and legs; swivel head; hand-carved on foot "Raikes T001 '84."

Note the earlier method of identification was used on this prototype. The popular design of Jamie was reproduced by Applause in 1985 (Illustration 175). Courtesy of Cathy and Robert Raikes Sr.

Illustration 92. Sherwood (Prototype). Woody Bear. 1983. A Robert Raikes original. 14in (36cm) tall; short dark brown acrylic fur; hand-carved wooden face and foot pads; hand-painted freckles; inset plastic eyes; jointed arms and legs; swivel head; hand-carved on foot "Raikes '83 SS014;" label on leg "Raikes Original Woody Bear."

Raikes' popular design of Sherwood was reproduced by Applause in 1985 (Illustration 176). Courtesy of Cathy and Robert Raikes Sr.

Illustration 94. Woody Bear. 1984. A Robert Raikes original. 21in (53cm) tall; long silky smokey blue acrylic fur; hand-carved wooden face and foot pads; inset plastic eyes; jointed arms and legs; swivel head; hard-stuffed body; hand-carved on foot "84 Raikes L21;" hand-signed in gold ink "Robert Raikes."

One-of-a-kind. Collector gave Bob the beautiful material to make this bear. In the majority of the early bears, hand-carved "wooden pads" were only used on the feet. Courtesy of Peter and Janice Spitzer.

ABOVE LEFT: Illustration 95. Roller Skater. *Woody Bear. 1984. A Robert Raikes original. 15in (38cm) tall; black acrylic fur; hand-carved wooden face and foot pads; inset plastic eyes; jointed arms and legs; swivel head; hard-stuffed body; hand-carved wooden roller skates; hand-carved on foot "Raikes '84 M144."*

Approximately ten in the edition. Courtesy of Cathy and Robert Raikes Sr.

ABOVE RIGHT: Illustration 96. Pirate. *Woody Bear. 1984. A Robert Raikes original. 16in (40cm) tall; black with gray fleck acrylic fur; hand-carved wooden face, feet and paw pads; inset plastic eyes; hard-stuffed body; jointed arms and legs; swivel head; hand-carved on foot "Raikes '84 M153;" hand-written in gold ink "Raikes;" cloth tag on leg "Raikes Original Woody Bear." Hand-carved wooden sword; metal hook screwed into paw; black patch over eye; black and tan cotton turban.*

Approximately ten Raikes' Pirates were made between 1984 and 1986. Note how soon Robert Raikes began creating variations to his original Woody Bear *design.* Courtesy of Peter and Janice Spitzer.

"I only made about three gnomes. The first (1976) was all carved in wood playing a pan flute (*Illustration 15*). He was only 8in (20cm) tall. The next (1979) carried a cane and a pipe (*Illustration 40*). The last gnome I made was in 1983.

"I originally designed the doll Molly as a Christmas present for my mother. It was also one of my favorite dolls (*Illustration 68*). Created in 1985, I later made about three different versions of this cute little girl doll. My mother also persuaded me to make her a baby doll (*Illustration 67*). Molly and Baby were the designs used for the first series of Raikes dolls manufactured by Applause (*Illustration 206*).

"I created two different styles of Little Red Riding Hood with a wolf. Each Red Riding Hood came with a very realistic-looking hand-carved wooden wolf doll. One version of wolf was all-wood and the other had a cloth body (*Illustration 70*).

"I made five different creations of Goldilocks. The bears were sold separately.

"In 1983, I designed a very scary-looking witch to exhibit at a doll show. She had lots of character with intricately carved features. Her body was cloth, with carved wooden hands and feet. Dressed in black, she carried a bundle of sticks and held a carved wooden apple with a worm crawling out of it (*Illustration 58*).

"I produced about 25 clowns from 1977 to 1986. All were different. The majority had cloth bodies and were 24in (61cm) tall. In 1984, I made a Medieval Jester doll (*Illustration 59*). It was all-wood, with articulated head and body. Even the wrists were jointed. It was a fun doll to design and make.

"The big-eyed (large painted eyes) series of dolls were made from 1981 to 1982 (*Illustration 43*). Approximately 12 were produced. I was exploring the limits of expression.

"I also remember making three Prairie Women, two Indians, one boy skier (*Illustration 73*) and a queen doll. I am sure there are many other designs I haven't mentioned, as collectors would give me unusual requests, and I like nothing more than the challenge of creating something new."

The vigorous and dedicated young sculptor crams as much as he can into life. He looks at each new piece he carves as a learning process that takes him into the next level. This is how he comes up with so many ideas; he never dwells

RIGHT: Illustration 99. *The "Raikes Originals Woody Bear" certificate of authenticity accompanied each bear Robert Raikes produced. The number of that particular bear and the date it was made was handwritten on the certificate. This version of a certificate was used until 1986, when it appears it was changed in 1987 to the example in* Illustration 132. *This is the original certificate for the* Jester *bear in* Illustration 97. Courtesy of Peter and Janice Spitzer.

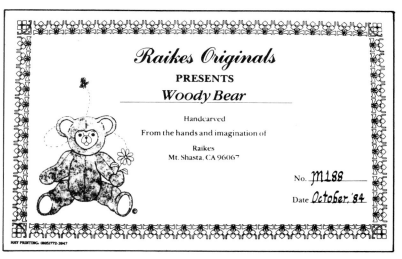

Raikes Originals

P.O. Box 82
Mt. Shasta, CA 96067
(916) 926-5607

Illustration 98. *Example of the hand-tag that was attached to Robert Raikes' Woody Bears. Courtesy of Cathy and Robert Raikes Sr.*

Illustration 97. *Jester. Woody Bear. 1984. A Robert Raikes original. 16in (41cm) tall; beige acrylic fur; hand-carved wooden face and foot pads; hand-painted face; inset plastic eyes; jointed arms and legs; swivel head; hard-stuffed body; hand-carved on foot "Raikes '84 M188." Dressed as a jester in pale and medium shades of lavender satin. Colors coordinate with painted face.*

With the success of Robert Raikes' clown dolls, it was only natural for him to create bears with hand-painted clown faces. Each bear came with its own certificate of authenticity (Illustration 99). Courtesy of Peter and Janice Spitzer.

Illustration 101. Woody Bear. *1984. A Robert Raikes original. 19in (48cm) tall; light beige acrylic fur; hand-carved wooden face and foot pads; inset plastic eyes; hand-painted freckles on snout; jointed arms and legs; hard-stuffed body; hand-carved on foot "Raikes '84 L280." Dressed in lavender and white apron and white bonnet.*

One of the earlier "hard-stuffed" designs. Courtesy of Molly Bakkum.

ABOVE: Illustration 100. Woody Bear. *1984. A Robert Raikes original. 20in (50cm) tall; long dark brown acrylic fur; hand-carved wooden face and foot pads; inset plastic eyes; jointed arms and legs; swivel head; hard-stuffed body; hand-carved on foot "Raikes '84 L210." Dressed in gray, black and beige tweed vest, beige tie.*

Good example of one of the early hard-stuffed designs. Note how quickly Robert Raikes developed a very unique and professional look with his bears. It appears hand-carved wooden pads were only used on the feet on the early designs. Courtesy of Cathy and Robert Raikes Sr.

ABOVE: Illustration 102. Woody Bear. *1984. A Robert Raikes original. Approximately 18in (46cm) tall; black acrylic fur; hand-carved wooden face and foot pads; inset plastic eyes; jointed arms and legs; swivel head; hard-stuffed body; signed and numbered on foot.*

Many of the early bears would be originally dressed with only a tie, bow or a bib. Photograph taken by Robert Raikes in the beautiful snow-covered mountains surrounding his Mount Shasta home. Courtesy of Robert and Carol Raikes.

ABOVE: Illustration 103. Faerie. Woody Bear. *Circa 1984. A Robert Raikes original. Approximately 14in (36cm) tall; dark gray variegated acrylic fur; hand-carved wooden face, wings and foot pads; inset plastic eyes; jointed arms and legs; swivel head; hard-stuffed body; hand-signed and numbered on foot.*

Very few Raikes Faerie bears were produced. With Robert Raikes' uncanny ability to bring fantasy to a tangible state and the tremendous response he received from his Faerie dolls, it was only natural he should design a Faerie bear. Courtesy of Robert and Carol Raikes.

Illustration 104. (Left) Woody Bear. *1984. A Robert Raikes original. 16in (41cm) tall; dark brown acrylic fur; hand-carved wooden face and foot pads; inset plastic eyes; hard-stuffed body; jointed arms and legs; swivel head; hand-carved on foot "Raikes '84 M119."*

Early "burned" wood method.
(Right) Woody Bear. *1984. A Robert Raikes original. 16in (41cm) tall; pale gray acrylic fur; hand-carved wooden face and foot pads; inset plastic eyes; hard-stuffed body; jointed arms and legs; swivel head; hand-carved on foot "Raikes '84 M207;" tag on leg "Raikes Original Woody Bear."*

Early versions of the popular Chelsea-face design. Courtesy of Peter and Janice Spitzer.

Illustration 107. Woody Bear. *1984. A Robert Raikes original. 10in (25cm) tall; all hand-carved wood; inset plastic eyes; jointed arms and legs; swivel head.*

One-of-a-kind experimental bear. Courtesy of Carol and Robert Raikes.

Illustration 106. *Pouty-face* Woody Bear. *1984. A Robert Raikes original. 12in (31cm) tall; beige acrylic fur; hand-carved wooden face and foot pads; hand-painted freckles and eyebrows; inset plastic eyes; jointed arms and legs; swivel head; hard-stuffed body; signed on foot.*

A good example of a Raikes popular "pouty-face" bear design. As a natural follow-up to the pouty-face dolls, Robert Raikes produced a number of different series of pouty-face bears from 1983 to 1988. Courtesy of Cathy and Robert Raikes Sr.

Illustration 105. Woody Bear. *1984. A Robert Raikes original. 21in (53cm) tall; black-tipped silver acrylic fur; hand-carved wooden face and foot pads; inset plastic eyes; hard-stuffed body; jointed arms and legs; swivel head; hand-carved on foot "Raikes '84 L304."*

Note hand-carved and painted heart on left side of face. Courtesy of Peter and Janice Spitzer.

BELOW: Illustration 108. *Masque-face* Ballerina. Woody Bear. *1984. A Robert Raikes original. 18in (46cm) tall; variegated light beige acrylic fur; hand-carved wooden face and foot pads; hand-painted masque-face; inset plastic eyes; jointed arms and legs; swivel head; hard-stuffed body; signed, dated and numbered on foot. Dressed in pink tulle tutu with flower (at ear).*

Very popular design. Came in several face styles and fabric colors. Approximately 50 were produced. Photographed by Robert Raikes in Mount Shasta, California. Courtesy of Robert and Carol Raikes.

ABOVE: Illustration 109. Jester. Woody Bear. *1984. A Robert Raikes original. Approximately 16in (41cm) tall; white acrylic fur; hand-carved wooden face and foot pads; inset plastic eyes; jointed arms and legs; swivel head; hand-signed, dated and numbered on foot. Dressed as a jester in a satin ruffle and hat.* Courtesy of Robert and Carol Raikes.

ABOVE: Illustration 110. Tyrone (Prototype). Woody Bear. *1984. A Robert Raikes original. 38in (97cm) tall; variegated gray acrylic fur; hand-carved wooden face, foot and paw pads; inset plastic eyes; jointed arms and legs; stationary head; hand-carved on foot "Raikes #1."*

When Bob decided to carve the prototype for Tyrone, he could not find a piece of kiln-dried wood thick enough to carve the face. So he went into the woods with his chain saw and cut down a dead Port Orford cedar tree that was still standing. He sliced it down to the size he needed, blocked it out and then carved it. To allow the wood to dry faster, he hollowed the face out from behind. Bob's father is the proud owner of this rare and dignified fellow. He proudly sits in the half-scale Model T car Bob's father built in 1953 for the children to drive in their town's parade. Approximately 20 Tyrones were produced between 1984 and 1986. Courtesy of Cathy and Robert Raikes Sr.

RIGHT: *Illustration 111. An example of the progression of Robert Raikes original bears. On the right is one of his first designs with the flatter snout, applied hand-carved wooden nose and painted eyes (1982). On the left we see how this creative artist's work developed a design of a bear (made in 1985) that has established him the recognition of being one of America's best-known and successful teddy bear artists of the 1980s-1990s.* Courtesy of Robert and Carol Raikes.

OPPOSITE PAGE: *Illustration 113. One of the photographs Robert Raikes would mail to his collectors showing the variety of bears available at that particular time (circa 1984). Note the dark finish to the wood on some of the bears.* Courtesy of Robert and Carol Raikes.

Illustration 112. Santa. Woody Bear. 1984. *A Robert Raikes original. Approximately 22in (56cm) tall; dark brown acrylic fur; hand-carved wooden face and foot pads; inset plastic eyes; spun glass beard; jointed arms and legs; swivel head; hand-signed, dated and numbered on foot.*

Robert Raikes designed approximately four different designs of Santa bears. One was the size of Tyrone 36in (91cm) tall. Two were designs for Applause (Illustrations 200 and 208). Courtesy of Robert and Carol Raikes.

Illustration 114. Swiss Girl. Woody Bear. *1985. A Robert Raikes original. 24in (56cm) tall; cream-colored acrylic fur; hand-carved wooden face, feet and paw pads; hand-painted paw design; inset plastic eyes; jointed arms and legs; swivel head; hand-carved on foot "Raikes LS079;" label on leg "Raikes Original Woody Bear." Dressed in red pinafore, white blouse and dark blue scarf.*

Rebecca-face. Note hand-carved wooden paw pads were now being used on a large percentage of the bears. Also, we see hand-painted foot design is added to some of the bears. This facial design was reproduced by Applause as Rebecca in the first edition in 1985. The oil painting of Raikes' Rebecca by Applause is on canvas and was painted by Pat Woodman. Courtesy of Robert and Pat Woodman. Photograph by Robert Woodman.

Illustration 115. *(Left)* Jamie. Woody Bear. *1985. A Robert Raikes original. 11in (28cm) tall; brown acrylic fur; hand-carved wooden face and foot pads; hand-painted freckles on snout; inset plastic eyes; jointed arms and legs; swivel head; hand-written on foot in brown ink "41 Raikes '85."*

(Center) Jamie. Woody Bear. *1988. A Robert Raikes original. 12in (28cm) tall; tan wool; hand-carved wooden face and foot pads; hand-painted freckles on snout; inset plastic eyes; jointed arms and legs; swivel head; hand-written in brown ink "Robert Raikes 1988."*

(Right) Jamie. Woody Bear. *1985. A Robert Raikes original. 12in (28cm) tall; black variegated gray acrylic fur; hand-carved wooden face and foot pads; hand-painted freckles on snout; inset plastic eyes; jointed arms and legs; swivel head; hand-written on foot in brown ink "39 Raikes '85."*

Three versions of Robert Raikes' Jamie.
Courtesy of Peter and Janice Spitzer.

on one piece. He can hardly wait to complete a design as he is always anxious to move on to the next idea.

The road from "birds to bears" was not an easy one for the persevering young sculptor. But in 1982, when Bob decided to venture into the growing world of teddy bears, he found he had discovered a true winner. His was a brand new kind of teddy bear. Immediately recognizable by their appealing hand-carved wooden faces, they were marketed under the name of *Woody Bear*.

Speaking of his work, Bob says, "After all, bears come from the woods. Wood comes from the woods. And we all know Woody Bears come from the woods."

The enchanting faces of the Raikes bears were sculpted from "Oregon sugar pine," with high-quality synthetic fur bodies and jointed limbs. The bodies were stuffed with polyester fiberfill and had hand-carved wooden feet and paw pads. However, the majority of the early designs did not have carved wooden paw pads (*Illustration 89*). As the faces on the bears were carved, Bob felt the bodies should have more of a firm sculptured feeling. So he employed local high school football players to stuff the bodies. Bob changed this form of stuffing when the collectors requested he make the bodies softer and more cuddly.

The very first bears Bob made were quite primitive looking. At first, he experimented with carving most of the face including the ears (but not the nose) from one piece of wood, and then hand-painting the eyes. Unsure of how to carve the nose, Bob applied a separate sculptured small wood nose (*Illustration 81*). This rare and interesting example of Raikes' first bear's head would not have been saved had it not been for Robert Raikes Sr., who retrieved it from the trash where his son had discarded it the day before.

The artist's next attempt (1981) was a personal project of a little unjointed, plush teddy bear. It was a Christmas gift for his mother in 1981. As before, he hand-carved a similar face, but this time made the ears of plush as part of the head (*Illustration 82*).

Raikes made his first real serious teddy bear prototype in 1982. Here in *Illustration 83* we see a basic jointed teddy bear with the *Woody Bear* hand-carved wooden face starting to take shape.

The first design Bob made for resale had many of his experimental characteristics with the small applied sculptured nose. However, he changed the eyes to yellow plastic (not inset) and added hand-carved wooden foot pads (*Illustration 84*). Produced in 1983, there were only approximately ten of this design.

Just as it was with his dolls, it was not long before the talented artist created a more professional and appealing-looking bear. He quickly mastered the problem with the nose by learning to carve the entire face from one piece of wood and insetting the eyes (*Illustration 89*).

Illustration 118. Woody Bear. 1985. A Robert Raikes original. 23in (58cm) tall; dark brown acrylic fur; hand-carved "redwood" face, feet and paws; inset plastic eyes; jointed arms and legs; swivel head; hand-carved on foot "Raikes '85 LS095."

Robert Raikes experimented by using redwood, but found it a difficult medium in which to work. He produced approximately two dolls in redwood, one of which was an Indian, and approximately 20 bears. Note the stenciled foot design. Courtesy of Peter and Janice Spitzer.

LEFT: Illustration 116. Panda. Woody Bear. 1985. A Robert Raikes original. 24in (61cm) tall; black and white acrylic fur; hand-carved wooden face, foot and paw pads; hand-painted face, foot and paw pads; inset plastic eyes; jointed arms and legs; swivel head; hand-carved on foot "1985 R. Raikes #3."

Robert Raikes produced several small editions of pandas with different faces. Courtesy of Cathy and Robert Raikes Sr.

Illustration 117. (Left) Koala. Woody Bear. 1985. A Robert Raikes original. 15in (38cm) tall; gray and white acrylic fur; hand-carved wooden nose; black Ultrasuede foot and paw pads; inset plastic eyes; jointed arms and legs; swivel head.

One-of-a-kind experimental design. (Right) Koala. Woody Bear. 1986. A Robert Raikes original. 16in (41cm) tall; gray and white acrylic fur; hand-carved wooden nose, foot and paw pads; hand-painted black nose, foot and paw pads; plastic eyes; jointed arms and legs; swivel head; hand-carved on foot "'85 Raikes 3."

Approximately 15 were produced of this koala design. At this writing, this is the only edition of koalas Robert Raikes produced. Courtesy of Cathy and Robert Raikes Sr.

RIGHT:Illustration 120. Woody Bear. *1986. A Robert Raikes original. 23in (58cm) tall; snowy white silky acrylic fur; hand-carved wooden face, feet and paw pads; hand-painted foot design; inset plastic eyes; jointed arms and legs; swivel head; hand-carved on foot "Raikes" 1986 Robert Raikes 1-25;" label on leg "Raikes Original Woody Bear."*

The hand-painted mask on the face adds so much character to the bear. Courtesy of Peter and Janice Spitzer.

Illustration 119. Woody Bear. *1985. A Robert Raikes original. 18in (46cm) tall; variegated dark gray acrylic fur; hand-carved wooden face, foot and paw pads; inset plastic eyes; jointed arms and legs; swivel head; hand-carved on foot "Raikes MS064;" hand-signed in black ink "Robert Raikes 1985."*

Note Chelsea-face. This facial design was reproduced by Applause as Chelsea *in the first edition in 1985 (Illustration 173).* Courtesy of Colleen Fontana.

Illustration 121. *Six months of hard work are shown here in the Raikes hand-carved heads awaiting to be assembled into adorable* Woody Bears. Courtesy of Robert and Carol Raikes.

Bob improved upon another early method of work. Instead of burning the wood with a blowtorch to obtain the look he wanted (*Illustration 91*), he was able to accomplish a realistic effect by allowing the natural grain of the wood to show through (*Illustration 126*). After the features are carved, sanded and painted, the wood is finished with a clear protective coat. In some cases, a little pigment was added to the lacquer to give it color and depth (*Illustration 113*). Freckles were also painted on the face and a stenciled foot design on the feet was an additional attraction on some of the bears (*Illustration 126*).

Bob also experimented with carving in redwood (*Illustration 118*), but found it a difficult medium in which to work, so there were very few of these bears made.

Every bear was hand-carved, signed, dated and numbered on the foot and came with its own certificate of authenticity (*Illustration 99*). Most of the bears were signed "Robert Raikes," "R.W. Raikes" or "Raikes." Bob almost always hand-carved the identification marks and his signature (*Illustration 90*), but in some instances he used a permanent ink pen. A percentage also came with a cloth tag sewn into the leg with the name "Raikes Original Woody Bear" on the label. In addition, the "Woody Bear, Raikes Originals" hang tag was tied to the arm of the bear. Each bear was an original. However, the bears were made in a series of limited editions.

The majority of the editions were limited to 25 or 30. Unless there was a special one-of-a-kind bear or a prototype, most of the bears were numbered.

Originally, they were hand-signed, dated and numbered in black ink. It appears the numbers did not signify the number of the bears made as approximately only ten of this early design were produced (*Illustration 85*). Also marked on the bear's foot were the letters indicating the size: "T.B.," "S.B.," "M.B." or "B.B.," meaning tiny, small, medium or big bear (*Illustration 85*). With the introduction of a new design where the bear's face was now carved entirely from one piece of wood, the identification system changed. For example, "Raikes '84 M188." This indicated the bear was medium size, number 188, made in 1984. In approximately 1985, when the "firm" stuffing of the bears was changed to the "soft," more cuddly variety, the letters were changed slightly to "SS," "MS" or "LS," which simply implied the body now had soft stuffing. For example, "Raikes MS032 '85" indicated the bear was medium size, softly stuffed, number 32, made in 1985.

As I stated earlier, the majority of the bears were made in editions. In 1986, the identification system was changed yet again, to inform the collectors of the number in the edition of that particular bear. The letters indicating the size "SS," "MS" and "LS" were deleted. Now the bears were marked with the edition as well as the number of that specific bear. For example, "Raikes 7/25 '86" clearly

Illustration 122. *Panda. Woody Bear. 1986. A Robert Raikes original. 24in (61cm) tall; silky black and white acrylic fur; hand-carved wooden face, feet and paw pads; hand-painted black and white face; inset plastic eyes; jointed arms and legs; swivel head; hand-carved on foot "R. W. Raikes 1986 #7;" hand-signed in gold ink "Robert Raikes."*

Several small editions of Raikes' pandas were produced with different faces. This panda was the second design made. Courtesy of Peter and Janice Spitzer.

Illustration 123. *Baby Woody Bears. Circa 1986. A Robert Raikes original. Approximately 12in (31cm) tall; (Left) beige acrylic fur; (Right) dark brown acrylic fur; Ultrasuede inner ears, foot and paw pads; hand-carved wooden snout; hand-painted freckles and features; plastic eyes; jointed arms and legs; stationary head.*

Experimental bears. Approximately four or five different versions of Raikes' Baby Woody Bears were produced in very small editions. Courtesy of Robert and Carol Raikes.

Illustration 125. (Left) Woody Bear. 1986. A Robert Raikes original. 18in (46cm) tall; black acrylic fur; hand-carved face, feet and foot pads; inset plastic eyes; jointed arms and legs; swivel head; hand-carved on foot "4/25 Raikes 1986." Dressed in pink and white "party dress" with matching bow (at ear).

Note Chelsea-face. Another edition of this popular sweet-face design.
(Middle Left) Pouty-face Ballerina. Woody Bear. 1985. A Robert Raikes original. 18in (46cm) tall; cream-colored acrylic fur; hand-carved wooden face, feet and paw pads; inset plastic eyes; jointed arms and legs; swivel head; hand-carved on foot "Raikes '85 MS032." Dressed in pink tulle tutu and pink rose (at ear).

Outfits were also available in pastel shades of mint green, lavender and yellow.
(Middle Right) Sailor. Woody Bear. 1985. A Robert Raikes original. 18in (46cm) tall; brown acrylic fur; hand-carved wooden face, feet and paw pads; hand-painted freckles on snout; inset plastic eyes; jointed arms and legs; swivel head; hand-carved on foot "Raikes '85 MS 028." Dressed in white and blue sailor suit.
(Right) Pouty-face Woody Bear. 1986. A Robert Raikes original. 18in (46cm) tall; snowy white acrylic fur; hand-carved face, feet and paws; inset plastic eyes; jointed arms and legs; swivel head; hand-carved on foot "Robert Raikes 2/25 1986." Dressed in knitted dark blue and white scarf and hat, with the words "Woody Bear" knitted into scarf.

Example of the four outfits the 18in (46cm) tall original Raikes Woody Bears were dressed in during 1985 to 1986. Courtesy of Peter and Janice Spitzer.

Illustration 124. Baby Bear. Woody Bear. 1986. A Robert Raikes original. 16in (41cm) tall; pale cinnamon-colored acrylic fur; pale beige Ultrasuede inner ears; hand-carved wooden face, feet and paw pads; inset plastic eyes; jointed arms and legs; swivel head; hand-carved on foot "R. W. Raikes 1986 #5."

Baby Bear was originally created in celebration of Linda Mullins' 1986 San Diego Teddy Bear, Doll and Antique Toy Festival where Robert Raikes appeared as a celebrity guest. Approximately 21 were in the edition. A small percentage had cry boxes encased in body. They came in a variety of colors and furs. Some had hand-painted freckles on face. Note the unusual design of the carved wooden face and chunky baby body. Courtesy of Francine Ferris.

Illustration 126. (Left) Swiss Girl. Woody Bear. 1986. A Robert Raikes original. 23in (58cm) tall; dark brown acrylic fur; hand-carved wooden face, feet and paw pads; hand-painted foot design and freckles on snout; inset plastic eyes; jointed arms and legs; swivel head; hand-carved on foot "Raikes '86 14-25;" label on leg "Raikes Original Woody Bear." Dressed in maroon dress and scarf, white blouse, maroon and white print apron.

(Center) Ballerina. Woody Bear. 1987. A Robert Raikes original. 23in (58.4cm) tall; snowy white acrylic fur; hand-carved wooden face (smiling), feet and paw pads; hand-painted freckles on face and foot design; inset plastic eyes; jointed arms and legs; swivel head; hand-carved on foot "1987 Robert Raikes 14/25." Dressed in pink tulle tutu and pink rose (at ear).

(Right) Country Girl. Woody Bear. 1986. A Robert Raikes original. 23.5in (60cm) tall; black acrylic fur; hand-carved wooden face, feet and paw pads; hand-painted freckles and foot design; inset plastic eyes; jointed arms and legs; swivel head; hand-carved on foot "'86 Raikes 11/25;" label on leg "Raikes Original Woody Bear." Dressed in blue and pink print dress and matching bonnet, white apron.

Example of the outfits in which Raikes 23in (58cm) tall girl bears were dressed during 1987 to 1988. Courtesy of Peter and Janice Spitzer.

Illustration 127. Tyrone. Woody Bear. 1986. A Robert Raikes original. 38in (97cm) tall; pale gray acrylic fur; hand-carved wooden face, feet and paw pads; inset plastic eyes; jointed arms and legs; stationary head; hand-carved on foot "'86 Raikes #13."

Note dark effect given to wood. Rare Scotsman outfit. The majority of Tyrones are dressed in tuxedos. Courtesy of Peter and Janice Spitzer.

Illustration 128. The Artist Woody Bear was one of Bob's favorites. He said he had fun smearing different colors of paint over parts of the fur. Circa 1987. 15in (38cm) tall. Approximately four Raikes' Artist bears were produced. Courtesy of Robert and Carol Raikes.

Illustration 129. (Left) *Boy. Woody Bear. 1987. A Robert Raikes original. 23in (58cm) tall; light beige acrylic fur; hand-carved wooden face, feet and paw pads; hand-painted foot design; inset plastic eyes; jointed arms and legs; swivel head; hand-carved on foot "Robert Raikes 1987 24/25." Dressed in brown check waistcoat with beige tie.*

(Center) Girl. Woody Bear. 1987. A Robert Raikes original. 23in (58cm) tall; dark brown acrylic fur; hand-carved wooden face, feet and paw pads; hand-painted foot design; inset plastic eyes; jointed arms and legs; swivel head; hand-carved on foot "Robert Raikes 6/25 1987." Dressed in pink and white striped dress with white cotton pinafore.

(Right) Pouty-face Boy. Woody Bear. 1986. A Robert Raikes original. 22in (56cm) tall; snowy white acrylic fur; hand-carved wooden face, feet and paw pads; inset plastic eyes; jointed arms and legs; swivel head; hand-carved on foot "Raikes 14/25 '86." Dressed in black velvet tuxedo, white shirt, white satin vest and black bow tie.
Courtesy of Peter and Janice Spitzer.

informed the collector this bear was number seven in an edition of 25 made in 1986.

The only problem with the numbering system that concerned Bob was the collectors might not realize each bear was an original piece, only similar within the series. Take for example, the *Ballerina*. All were dressed like ballerinas with painted faces, but each bear's clothes and face were slightly modified.

The popularity of the bears increased to such an extent that soon the Raikes stopped producing so many dolls and concentrated on creating teddy bears.

Bob and Carol were already working long hours on the dolls. So, when they decided to produce bears, Bob approached his brother, Mike, and his wife, Cindy, with the idea of helping with the bears in their spare time, on a "profit sharing" basis. Mike was a wood shop teacher at Mount Shasta High School, and the "profit sharing" agreement made sense to him.

Mike assembled the parts and stuffed the bears after Cindy made the bodies. Bob told the humorous story of how his brother's house soon began to resemble his own as he was initiated into the *Woody Bear* business. "There he was, with a whole room stuffed full of fur and polyfill, stuffing 'Woodies' like mad every night till midnight," Bob said laughingly. It is difficult at first for anyone to comprehend the terrific amount of energy that goes into a project like this.

Bob was constantly working on new and original designs. The public response to Raikes' *Woody Bears* was nothing short of sensational. His fame spread fast, establishing him as one of America's best-known and respected original teddy bear artists and sculptors of the 1980s.

When asked if he felt his bears were people, Bob replied, "Bears are bears, and people are people. Rather, I see them as extensions of our personalities. In that respect I think they are mirrors of our humanity. In the same way a child wants a teddy bear for warmth and security, adults find in teddy bears reflections of the better nature of man...for adults, something very important to hold onto."

As with his dolls, the creative artist made numerous appealing designs of bears.

As a natural follow-up to the pouty-face dolls, Bob produced a series of pouty-face bears (*Illustration 106*). Another popular design was the *Ballerina*

Illustration 130. (*Left*) Train Engineer. Woody Bear. *1987. A Robert Raikes original. 22in (56cm) tall; variegated black and gray acrylic fur; hand-painted freckles on snout and foot design; inset plastic eyes; jointed arms and legs; swivel head; hand-carved on foot "Robert Raikes 1987 5/25." Dressed in blue and white striped engineer overalls and cap, red and white scarf.*
(*Center*) Country Boy. Woody Bear. *1986. A Robert Raikes original. 23in (58cm) tall; pale beige acrylic fur; hand-carved wooden face, feet and paw pads; hand-painted freckles and foot design; inset plastic eyes; jointed arms and legs; swivel head; hand-carved on foot "R W Raikes 1986 1/25;" label on leg "Raikes Original Woody Bear." Dressed in blue denim overalls and pale blue shirt.*

This design of face was reproduced by Applause as Sebastian in their first edition in 1985.
(*Right*) Swiss Boy. Woody Bear. *1986. A Robert Raikes original. 23in (58cm) tall; brown and variegated beige acrylic fur; hand-carved wooden face, feet and paw pads; hand-painted freckles and foot design; inset plastic eyes; jointed arms and legs; swivel head; hand-written in gold ink on foot "1986 Robert Raikes 7-25." Dressed in brown lederhosen and white shirt. Courtesy of Peter and Janice Spitzer.*

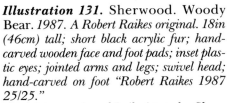

Illustration 131. Sherwood. Woody Bear. *1987. A Robert Raikes original. 18in (46cm) tall; short black acrylic fur; hand-carved wooden face and foot pads; inset plastic eyes; jointed arms and legs; swivel head; hand-carved on foot "Robert Raikes 1987 25/25."*

A later version of Raikes' popular Sherwood design. Note no hand-carved wooden paw pads are used on Sherwood. Courtesy of Robert and Pat Woodman. Photograph by Robert Woodman.

BELOW: *Illustration 132. It appears this Robert Raikes certificate of authenticity was introduced in 1987 and was used for the Raikes dolls and the Woody Bears. Courtesy of Peter and Janice Spitzer.*

BELOW: Illustration 136. *Ballerina. Woody Bear. 1987. A Robert Raikes original. 20in (51cm) tall; white acrylic fur; hand-carved wooden face, feet and paw pads; inset plastic eyes; jointed arms and legs; swivel head; signed on foot. Dressed in pink tulle tutu and flower (at ear).*

This is the only **Ballerina** *Robert Raikes made with this facial design. It is also one of the artist's favorite bears. Courtesy of Robert and Carol Raikes.*

Illustration 135. Joey. Woody Bear. *1987. A Robert Raikes original. 12in (31cm) tall; short light brown acrylic fur; hand-carved wooden face and foot pads; inset plastic eyes; unjointed arms and legs; stationary head; hand-carved on foot "1987 Robert Raikes 5-50." Courtesy of Robert and Pat Woodman. Photograph by Robert Woodman.*

ABOVE: Illustration 133. Masque-face. Woody Bear. *1987. A Robert Raikes original. 60in (152cm) tall; black acrylic fur; hand-carved wooden face, feet and paw pads; hand-painted foot and paw designs on pads; hand-painted clown face; inset plastic eyes; jointed arms and legs; swivel head; hand-carved on foot "Robert Raikes;" numbered on certificate "1 of 1." Dressed in dark green velvet jacket with gold lamé collar and silver lamé bow tie.*

One-of-a-kind. Beautiful hand-painted face. Courtesy of Gene Zion.

Illustration 134. Kevi. Woody Bear. *1987. A Robert Raikes original. 14in (36cm) tall; golden brown acrylic fur; hand-carved wooden face and foot pads; hand-painted eyes; unjointed arms and legs; stationary head; hand-signed and numbered on foot.*

The concept for the **Kevi** *bear came to Bob after he had met the internationally acclaimed singer and entertainer Kevin Roth. Bob was so impressed by the children's response to Kevin and his singing that he had the idea to make a bear with a tape recording of Kevin's singing accompanying the bear. Applause reproduced the original Raikes* **Kevi** *bear with a tape recording of Kevin Roth singing. (For more information, refer to Illustration 199). However, Raikes' original* **Kevi** *does not include a tape. Courtesy of Robert and Carol Raikes.*

Illustration 138. *(Top left) Girl. Woody Bear. 1987. A Robert Raikes original. 17in (43cm) tall; long cream-colored acrylic fur; hand-carved wooden face, feet and paw pads; inset plastic eyes; jointed arms and legs; swivel head; hand-carved on foot "Robert Raikes 1987 17-25." Dressed in white and lavender nightdress and mop cap.*

(Top right) Girl. Woody Bear. 1988. A Robert Raikes original. 17in (43cm) tall; variegated brown acrylic fur; hand-carved wooden face, feet and paw pads; jointed arms and legs; swivel head; hand-written in brown ink "1988 Robert Raikes 12/25." Dressed in blue pinafore with blue and white blouse with matching bow (at ear).

Chelsea-*face.*

(Bottom left) Boy. Woody Bear. 1987. A Robert Raikes original. 18in (46cm) tall; long cream-colored acrylic fur; hand-carved wooden face, feet and paw pads; inset plastic eyes; jointed arms and legs; swivel head; hand-carved on foot "Robert Raikes 1987 7-25." Dressed in brown wool pants, white shirt and brown bow tie.

(Bottom center) Boy. Woody Bear. 1987. A Robert Raikes original. 18in (46cm) tall; long gray and black variegated acrylic fur; hand-carved wooden face, feet and paw pads; hand-painted freckles on snout; inset plastic eyes; jointed arms and legs; swivel head; hand-carved on foot "R. Raikes 1987 8/25." Dressed in gray and black flecked vest with rust-colored tie.

(Bottom right) Girl. Woody Bear. 1988. A Robert Raikes original. 17in (43cm) tall; light gray acrylic fur; hand-carved wooden face, feet and paw pads; hand-painted freckles on snout; inset plastic eyes; jointed arms and legs; swivel head; hand-carved on foot "1988 Robert Raikes 12-25." Dressed as a Swiss baby girl in a maroon dress with white lace bonnet.

Example of the outfits in which the 17in (43cm) tall bears were dressed in during 1987 and 1988. Courtesy of Peter and Janice Spitzer.

Illustration 139. Mother's Day *(Prototype)*. Woody Bear. *1988. A Robert Raikes original. 17in (42cm) tall; light beige acrylic fur; hand-carved wooden face, feet and paw pads; inset plastic eyes; jointed arms and legs; swivel head; hand-signed in brown ink "Robert Raikes' Mother's Day Prototype."*

Heart-shaped face with hand-painted freckles. Dressed in rose pink and floral dress and bow (at ear). Applause reproduced Raikes' Mother's Day *bear in 1989 (Illustration 204).* Courtesy of Peter and Janice Spitzer.

Illustration 137. Sherwood. Woody Bear. *1987. A Robert Raikes original. 16in (41cm) tall; beige acrylic fur; hand-carved wooden face and foot pads; hand-painted freckles on snout; inset plastic eyes; jointed arms and legs; swivel head.*

Experimental design of Sherwood. Courtesy of Peter and Janice Spitzer.

BELOW:Illustration 142. Faerie Rabbit. *1984. A Robert Raikes original. 19in (48cm) tall; all hand-carved wood; articulated head and body; hand-painted body and features; whiskers; hand-signed and dated. Dressed as a faerie in rose-colored leaf-shaped silk flowers.*

The highly collectible and very rare Faerie Rabbits are fine examples of the detail and creativity of Robert Raikes' work. Note the hand-painted body. Courtesy of Robert and Carol Raikes.

ABOVE: Illustration 141. *Miniature* Woody Bears. *1988. Robert Raikes original. 8in (20cm) tall; various shades of brown acrylic fur; hand-carved wooden face and foot pads; hand-painted eyes and features; jointed arms and legs; swivel head; signed on foot.*

Experimental bears. Approximately ten were made. Note seated bear has felt foot pads. Courtesy of Robert and Carol Raikes.

ABOVE: Illustration 140. *(Left)* Emily. Woody Bear. *1988. A Robert Raikes original. 24in (61cm) tall; light gray acrylic fur; hand-carved wooden face, feet and paw pads; inset plastic eyes; jointed arms and legs; swivel head; hand-carved on foot "1988 Robert Raikes 11-30." Attired in pink print dress with pale pink collar. Dress varies throughout the edition.*

(Center) Jason. Woody Bear. *1988. A Robert Raikes original. 1988. 18in (46cm) tall; beige acrylic fur; hand-carved wooden face, feet and paw pads; inset plastic eyes; jointed arms and legs; swivel head; hand-carved on foot "1988 Robert Raikes 21-25." Dressed in a hand-knitted sweater, velvet cap and bow tie.*

(Right) Jenny *(Prototype).* Woody Bear. *1988. A Robert Raikes original. 18in (46cm) tall; beige acrylic fur; jointed arms and legs; swivel head; hand-carved on foot "1988 Robert Raikes Prototype." Outfitted in rust-colored dress with matching bow (at ear).*

Emily, Jason and Jenny were named after Robert Raikes' children. They were reproduced by Applause in the summer of 1988 sixth edition as the "Home Sweet Home Collection" (Illustration 196). Courtesy of Peter and Janice Spitzer.

bear. They came in several face styles and fabric colors. They were dressed in dainty tulle tutus and flower (at ear). These outfits were available in pastel shades of mint green, lavender, rose and yellow. Bob's favorite was a 24in (61cm) *Pouty Ballerina* bear in white plush with a pink tutu (*Illustration 136*).

In 1985, Bob experimented with several koala faces. There were approximately only 15 made (*Illustration 117*).

There were several small editions of pandas with different faces. The painted black and white faces were all extremely striking (*Illustration 116* and *122*). He also made one impressive looking panda the size of *Tyrone*, 38in (97cm) tall.

The *Artist* was another of his favorites. "I only made about four *Artist* bears, but they were fun to make, as I smeared different colored paint over parts of the plush." (*Illustration 128*.)

Bob experimented with making *Santa Bears*. Here again only four designs were made. One was quite large and came with a spun glass beard (*Illustration 112*).

Very popular and quite rare were Bob's *Pirates*. He made about ten between 1984 and 1986. They came with a hook in place of one paw and a patch over the right eye (*Illustration 96*).

When Bob created the prototype for his 38in (97cm) tall *Tyrone*, he could not find a piece of kiln-dried wood thick enough to carve the face. So he went into the woods with his chain saw and cut down a dead Port Orford cedar tree that was still standing. He sliced it down to the size he needed, blocked it out and then carved it. To allow the wood to dry faster, he hollowed the face out from behind.

Bob's father is the proud owner of this rare and dignified-looking fellow. He recalls the attention the bear would receive when he took him to shows for exhibit, especially when he would drive up with *Tyrone* riding in the front seat of the car. Now the bear is retired and has a place of honor in the Raikes Sr.'s home. He proudly sits in the half-scale Model T car Bob's father built in 1953 for the children to drive in their town's parades (*Illustration 110*).

I asked Bob what gives him ideas for his various characters. He smiled and replied, "Many of my designs represent my childhood memories. Growing up in the late 1950s and early 60s, I loved watching cowboy and Indian movies. Two of my favorite stars were Roy Rogers and Dale Evans. That is where the idea for Bonnie and Jesse (the cowgirl and cowboy I designed for Applause) came from (*Illustration 202*).

"Then there was Engineer Bill. I feel my Train Engineer was a perfect interpretation of that popular celebrity and proved to be one of my most popular designs. I produced a few at a time between 1984 and 1988. I always varied the faces and the plush. And each engineer came with a train logo." (*Illustration 203*.)

The concept for the *Kevi* bear came to Bob after he had met the internationally acclaimed singer and entertainer Kevin Roth at the Hobby Center Toys, Doll and Teddy Bear Show in Toledo, Ohio. Bob was so impressed by the children's response to Kevin and his singing that Bob conceived the idea to make a bear with a tape recording of Kevin's singing accompanying the bear. After the show, Bob was at the airport waiting for his plane to arrive and he began to draw a couple of sketches of the *Kevi* bear. He said he was so excited about the idea, he could hardly wait to get to his studio the next morning to begin work on the prototype (*Illustrations 134* and *199*).

The idea for the painted-face clown dolls and bears originally came to be by unusual circumstances. Bob found a small imperfection or coloration in the wood on the face of a doll so rather than discard the piece, he came up with the notion to paint a design into that section, then make it symmetrical on the other side. The finished product was so stunning, and the creative artist so enjoyed the challenge of something new, that he produced a variety of clown dolls (*Illustration 50*) and small editions of clown bears between 1977 and 1986. On those *Ballerina* and *Jester* bears with slight discoloration in the wood, Bob would also artistically paint beautiful colored masks (*Illustration 97*).

Many of the names the artist chose for his bears were taken from the children of his secretary, seamstress and various friends. Bob suddenly realized he had never named his bears after any of his own children. So the bears in the Applause "Home Sweet Home Collection" (*Illustrations 197* and *198*) and Raikes

Illustration 143. Winged Faerie Rabbit. *1984. A Robert Raikes original. 10in (25cm) tall; all hand-carved wood; articulated head and body; hand-painted features; hand-signed and dated. Dressed as a faerie with gold wings and silk outfit in the shape of leaves.* Courtesy of Cathy and Robert Raikes Sr.

Illustration 144. Faerie Rabbit. *1984. A Robert Raikes original. 19in (48cm) tall; all hand-carved wood; articulated head and body; hand-painted features; whiskers; silk flower collar; hand-signed and dated.*

Approximately four of this design were produced. Courtesy of Robert and Carol Raikes.

Illustration 146. Bride and Groom. *Rabbits. 1984. Robert Raikes originals. 21in (53cm) tall; all hand-carved wood; articulated heads and bodies; hand-painted features; whiskers; hand-written on foot in black ink "R W Raikes '84." Dressed as a bride and groom.*

Only one set of the rabbits dressed as a bride and groom was produced. Courtesy of Cathy and Robert Raikes Sr.

Illustration 145. *An example of the all hand-carved wood, articulated head and body used for the Raikes* Faerie Rabbits. *A percentage of the rabbits were of natural wood and a few had painted bodies (Illustration 142).* Courtesy of Robert and Carol Raikes.

Illustration 147. *Rabbits. 1984. Robert Raikes originals. Approximately 21in (53cm) tall; all hand-carved wood; articulated heads and bodies; hand-painted eyes and features; whiskers; hand-signed. Dressed as a boy and girl.*

Sold in sets. Approximately 20 in edition. Courtesy of Robert and Carol Raikes.

Illustration 150. *Rabbits. 1986. Robert Raikes originals. 23in (58cm) tall; light beige acrylic fur; hand-carved wooden faces; sculptured beige Ultrasuede foot and paw pads; hand-painted eyes; whiskers; jointed arms and legs; swivel head; signed, dated and numbered in ink on foot. Girl dressed in pink dress with floral pinafore and pink bow (at ear). Boy dressed in black velvet vest and bow tie.*

Note these rabbits have jointed heads. The first Applause "plush" rabbits (Jill and Andrew) were made from this design (Illustration 192). Courtesy of Robert and Carol Raikes.

Illustration 149. *Rabbit. 1986. A Robert Raikes original. 21in (53cm) tall; green acrylic fur; gray Ultrasuede inner ears, foot and paw pads; hand-carved wooden face; hand-painted eyes; whiskers; jointed arms and legs; stationary head; hand-written in ink "Raikes '86." Dressed in a smart green velvet waistcoat with red silk rose on lapel.*

It appears this was the first design of Raikes' plush rabbits made for resale. Note the stationary head. The majority of the heads of Raikes' animals (excluding bears) were stationary. Courtesy of Peter and Janice Spitzer.

Illustration 151. *Rabbit. 1987. A Robert Raikes original. 24in (61cm) tall; pink acrylic fur; cream-colored Ultrasuede inner ears, foot and paw pads; hand-carved wooden face; hand-painted eyes; whiskers; jointed arms and legs; stationary head; hand-signed in black ink "1987 Raikes."*

One-of-a-kind. Courtesy of Peter and Janice Spitzer.

Illustration 148. *(Left) Rabbit. 1986. A Robert Raikes original. 21in (53cm) tall; short gray acrylic fur; Ultrasuede inner ear, foot and paw pads; hand-carved wooden face; hand-painted eyes; jointed arms and legs; stationary head.*

This design was used for the first edition of plush rabbits Robert Raikes produced. (Right) Rabbit. 1985. A Robert Raikes original. 15in (38cm) tall; long silky beige acrylic fur; beige Ultrasuede inner ear, foot and paw pads; hand-carved wooden face; hand-painted eyes; jointed arms and legs; stationary head.

First experimental design of a Raikes plush rabbit. Courtesy of Cathy and Robert Raikes Sr.

Illustration 154. *This is the first pig Bob designed. It stands 26in (66cm) tall and is unusual in that it has jointed arms, but the body consists of a square solid block of wood. The long country-style dress conceals the block body. Because of its design, it is very stable and can be used as a doorstop.* Courtesy of Robert and Carol Raikes.

Illustration 153. *Dog. 1985. A Robert Raikes original. 12in (31cm) tall; short brown acrylic fur; hand-carved wooden face, foot and paw pads; hand-painted foot and paw pads design; inset plastic eyes; jointed arms and legs; stationary head; carved wooden bone; hand-signed.*

Robert Raikes has created several designs of dogs in very small editions. However, this dog is a one-of-a-kind and at this writing, it has never been reproduced. Courtesy of Robert and Carol Raikes.

Illustration 155. *Original animals by Robert Raikes. 1985. Sizes range from 16in (41cm) tall to 20in (51cm) tall; various colors of acrylic fur; hand-carved faces.*

These were the prototypes of an experimental group of animals. The clothes were made by Applause. Courtesy of Robert and Carol Raikes.

Illustration 152. *Bunny. 1987. A Robert Raikes original. 9in (22cm) tall; pale beige acrylic fur; cream-colored Ultrasuede inner ears, foot and paw pads; hand-carved wooden face; hand-painted eyes; jointed arms and legs; stationary head; hand-signed in black ink "1987 Raikes 1-50."* Courtesy of Peter and Janice Spitzer.

Illustration 156. *(Left) Hedgehog. 1987. A Robert Raikes original. 15in (38cm) tall; variegated brown acrylic fur; hand-carved wooden face, paws and feet; inset plastic eyes; hand-painted features; jointed arms and legs; stationary head; hand-carved on foot "Robert Raikes 1987 1-50."*

Originally produced wearing a dress and cape.

(Center) Beaver. 1987. A Robert Raikes original. 16in (41cm) tall; dark brown acrylic fur; brown Ultrasuede tail and inner ear; hand-carved wooden face, teeth, paws and feet; inset plastic eyes; hand-painted features; jointed arms and legs, stationary head; hand-carved on foot "Robert Raikes 1987 13-50."

Originally produced with a matching jacket and hat.

(Right) Owl (Prototype). 1987. A Robert Raikes original. 12in (31cm) tall; variegated brown and white acrylic fur; hand-carved wooden face, beak and feet; inset plastic eyes; hand-painted features; jointed arms and legs; stationary head; hand-written on hang-tag "May 1987."

At this writing, the beaver, hedgehog and raccoon have been reproduced by Applause (Illustrations 193 and 207). Courtesy of Cathy and Robert Raikes Sr.

Illustration 157. *Monkey. 1987. A Robert Raikes original. 23in (58cm) tall; black acrylic fur; hand-carved wooden face, feet and hands; hand-painted brown eyes; jointed arms and legs; swivel head; posable tail; hand-carved on foot "1987 Robert Raikes 3-24."* Courtesy of Peter and Janice Spitzer.

Illustration 158. *Pigs. 1987. Robert Raikes originals. 23in (58cm) tall. Boy: short beige acrylic fur; light beige Ultrasuede inner ears; hand-carved wooden face and hooves; hand-painted brown eyes; jointed arms and legs; stationary head; hand-written on hoof in black ink "Robert Raikes #1 1987." Dressed in brown check pants, white shirt, brown waistcoat, brown check cap and bow tie. Girl: short pink acrylic fur; pale pink Ultrasuede in inner ears; hand-carved wooden face and hooves; hand-painted blue eyes; jointed arms and legs; stationary head; hand-signed in black ink on hoof "Robert Raikes #1 1987." Dressed in blue and white print blouse, pink and white striped skirt and apron, blue vest and pink mop cap.*

Edition of 20 pairs. Robert Raikes produced four different designs of pigs. Courtesy of Peter and Janice Spitzer.

originals of these designs (*Illustration 140*) were given his children's names, Jenny, Jason and Emily.

Over the years, Bob also created variations of beautiful rabbits — all hand-carved wood fairy rabbits (*Illustration 143*), all hand-carved wood articulated rabbits (*Illustration 147*) and plush rabbits (*Illustration 150*) in many sizes. These wonderful rabbits proved to be so popular, Bob went on to create many other outstanding animals.

Among Raikes' intriguing menagerie creations were hedgehogs, raccoons, owls and pigs.

Four different designs of pigs were produced. The first pig was 26in (66cm) tall and unusual in that it had jointed arms, but the body consisted of a square solid block of wood. A long country-style dress concealed the block body. Because of its design, it was very stable and could be used as a doorstop (*Illustration 154*).

The next pig Bob designed was a 6in (15cm) tall character wearing a country dress. In 1987, he introduced an edition of 23in (58cm) tall pigs. They came in pairs dressed as a boy and girl. There were approximately 20 pairs in this edition (*Illustration 158*).

There was only one style of hedgehog made. Dressed to look like a princess, she was designed to go with *Robin Raccoon*. However, they were sold separately. The hedgehog and the raccoon were made in an edition of 50 each.

To date, Bob has produced about 40 owls, 24 monkeys, 50 beavers and 50 bunnies. All the animals had jointed arms and legs and stationary heads, with the exception of the monkey. He was completely jointed with a posable tail (*Illustration 157*).

Although the Raikes had a thriving and successful bear-making business, Bob found he could not keep up the demand of his one-of-a-kind bears. Creating over 1200 original designs and exhibiting at 32 shows a year, he was already working at top production speed.

It was then he made the decision to approach the major gift company, Applause, to produce his designs. In the agreement, Bob was still able to produce special order bears under the name *Woody Bear*. However, on Bob's 40th birthday, October 13, 1987, the artist made the decision that a good portion of his original work will be produced for charitable organizations, special events and for members of the Robert Raikes Collector's Club. Since that time, his already valuable pieces have increased in value tremendously and are still climbing and extremely scarce.

Illustration 159. *Cat. 1989. A Robert Raikes original. 20in (51cm) tall; short pale cinnamon acrylic fur; hand-carved wooden face; Ultrasuede foot pads; inset green plastic eyes; jointed arms and legs; swivel head; hand-signed in black ink "Robert Raikes 4/49 1989."*

Dressed in turquoise dress with yellow print sleeves, matching hat and pink apron. Courtesy of Robert and Pat Woodman. Photograph by Robert Woodman.

Illustration 160. *Bob created these two outstanding bears for the 1990 Walt Disney World One-of-a-kind Teddy Bear Auction.* Hans *and* Gretchen *stand approximately 30in (76cm) high.* Hans *is dressed in classic lederhosen and* Gretchen *wears the traditional dirndl dress.* Courtesy of Applause, Inc.

Robert Raikes' Designs Find a Home With Applause

Applause, a world leader in the gift industry, is home to some of the best-known merchandising licenses in the country. The Woodland Hills, California, based company holds the rights to popular characters from Disney, Sesame Street, Warner Brothers (Looney Tunes and Tiny Toons), Universal MCA (American Tail), Dolls by Pauline and many more. More than 75,000 retailers nationwide purchase some of the most recognizable gift merchandise in the country from this thriving, privately-held company.

The original Wallace Berrie Company was founded in 1966. Wallace Berrie began as a supplier with a limited product line of novelty gifts. The company continued to expand over the next few years and in 1979, plush products represented a large percentage of their business.

In 1981, Larry Elins and Harris Toibb purchased the Wallace Berrie Company, and in August of the following year introduced a beautiful new line of realistic-looking animals.

Illustration 162. Attractively displayed is Max, *from the 1986 2nd Edition of Raikes Bears by Applause.* Courtesy of Applause, Inc.

Illustration 161. The designs of the Avanti line of animals produced by Applause faithfully replicate the detail of their real-life counterparts. Courtesy of Applause, Inc.

Illustration 165. The wood carvers in the Philippines use many carving tools for the intricate work on the faces of the Raikes Bears. Courtesy of Applause, Inc.

Illustration 163. A "Certificate of Authenticity" is enclosed in the collector's box with each limited edition Raikes Bear manufactured by Applause. Courtesy of Robert and Carol Raikes.

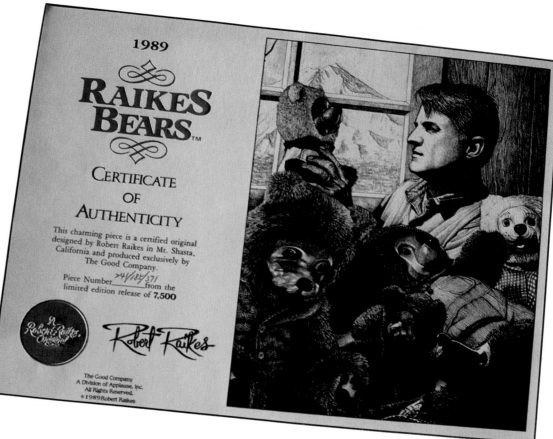

LEFT: *Illustration 164.* A carver hand-carves the face of the Raikes Bear design produced for Applause. The Phillipinos take great pride in their work as Applause sets high quality control on the Raikes products. Note how the craftsman works on three faces at once. Courtesy of Applause, Inc.

Illustration 166. This machine flap sands the carved wooden parts of the Raikes products. Courtesy of Applause, Inc.

Illustration 167. The carved wooden pieces for the Raikes animals are placed on racks to dry. Courtesy of Applause, Inc.

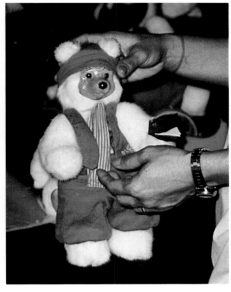

Illustration 170. An elf bear receives the final inspection before he is packaged and ready to be shipped to America. Courtesy of Applause, Inc.

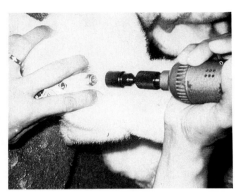

Illustration 169. The limbs of the Raikes animals are securely bolted together with an electric wrench. Courtesy of Applause, Inc.

Illustration 168. A group of the finished Raikes bear faces await assemblage. Courtesy of Applause, Inc.

Illustration 171.
Robert Raikes Creations by Applause
First Edition, Autumn 1985. Limited edition of 7500 of each design.
"From the hands of the artisan into your heart"
"A truly collectible series of fully jointed bears with finely carved wooden faces and paws of select cypress. Each Raikes Original is carefully detailed. Imbued with a distinct personality that is as unique as the intricately detailed clothing each wears.
"Individually signed and numbered, these Robert Raikes limited edition Originals come boxed with their own certificate of authenticity, ownership registration card and hang tag.
"It's easy to see why collectors have already expressed real interest in these fine pieces and why Raikes Originals are destined to become collector classics.
"The special creation of a special artist"
"Born in the visionary mind of artist and sculptor Robert Raikes, the design of each Raikes Bear takes shape in the sculptor's hands over countless hours.
"Attention to detail is the designer's forte. The wood used must have just the right color, grain and overall feel. The fur for each bear can be only the finest plush material. The result is a stunning work of art.
"Applause is proud to offer you the opportunity to acquire a very special and most distinctive limited edition bear. "A Robert Raikes Original."
(Raikes Collector Brochure, 1985.)

Illustration 172. *(Left)* Rebecca. *First Edition, Autumn 1985. Raikes Bear by Applause. 22in (56cm) tall; dark brown acrylic fur; carved wooden face and foot pads; inset plastic eyes; jointed arms and legs; swivel head; signed and numbered on foot; limited edition of 7500; style number 5447. "Wearing a two-piece dress with pinafore and satin ribbons. Rebecca is a very ladylike bear. She loves to be a trendsetter." (Raikes Collector Brochure, 1985.)*

(Right) Sebastian. *First Edition, Autumn 1985. Raikes Bear by Applause. 22in (56cm) tall; dark brown acrylic fur; carved wooden face and foot pads; inset plastic eyes; jointed arms and legs; swivel head; signed and numbered on foot; limited edition of 7500; style number 5445. "Peering at the world through wire spectacles, Sebastian wears a handsome plaid vest, velveteen bow tie and thinks of himself as dignified." (Raikes Collector Brochure, 1985.)* Courtesy of Robert and Carol Raikes.

Illustration 173. *(Left)* Bently. *First Edition, Autumn 1985. Raikes Bear by Applause. 14in (36cm) tall; charcoal-colored acrylic fur; carved wooden face and foot pads; inset plastic eyes; jointed arms and legs; swivel head; signed and numbered on foot; limited edition of 7500; style number 5448. "He's quite a proper fellow, Bently. His tweed vest with a pocket has a timeless quality and his outfit is topped off with a velveteen bow tie." (Raikes Collector Brochure, 1985.)*

(Center) Chelsea. *First Edition, Autumn 1985. Raikes Bear by Applause. 14in (36cm) tall; brown acrylic fur; carved wooden face and foot pads; inset plastic eyes; jointed arms and legs; swivel head; signed and numbered on foot; limited edition of 7500; style number 5451. "Dressed in an adorable rust and blue print dress with satin ribbons, she's everyone's little sweetheart." (Raikes Collector Brochure, 1985.)*

(Right) Eric. *First Edition, Autumn 1985. Raikes Bear by Applause. 14in (36cm) tall; dark brown acrylic fur; carved wooden face and foot pads; inset plastic eyes; jointed arms and legs; swivel head; signed and numbered on foot; limited edition of 7500; style number 5449. "Outfitted with a knitted sweater, hat and scarf (with 'Raikes Bears' knitted right into it), Eric's one true love is skiing." (Raikes Collector Brochure, 1985.)* Courtesy of Robert and Carol Raikes.

Illustration 174. (*Left*) Huckle Bear. *First Edition, August 1985. Raikes Bear by Applause. 22in (56cm) tall; gray acrylic fur; carved wooden face and foot pads; inset plastic eyes; jointed arms and legs; swivel head; signed and numbered on foot; limited edition of 7500; style number 5446.* "The farmer, Huckle Bear wears overalls with a real pocket that are perfect in every detail. He reads* Mark Twain *in his spare time."* (*Raikes Collector Brochure, 1985.*) *Seated to the right of Huckle Bear is Sherwood.* (*For further information on Sherwood, see Illustration 176.*) *Courtesy of Robert and Carol Raikes.*

Illustration 175. Jamie. *Autumn 1985. Raikes Bears by Applause. 10in (25cm) tall; (Left) gray acrylic fur; (Right) brown acrylic fur; carved wooden face and foot pads; inset plastic eyes; jointed arms and legs; swivel head; style number 5453.*

Unnumbered series. Jamie *was not manufactured with Robert Raikes' signature on the foot. The artist personally autographed these bears for the Woodmans at a teddy bear event.* Courtesy of Robert and Pat Woodman. Photograph by Robert Woodman.

Illustration 176. Sherwood. *Autumn 1985. Raikes Bear by Applause. 13in (33cm) tall; (Left) dark brown acrylic fur; (Right) light brown acrylic fur; carved wooden face and foot pads; inset plastic eyes; jointed arms and legs; swivel head; style number 5452.*

Unnumbered series. Sherwood *was not manufactured with Robert Raikes' signature on the foot. The artist personally autographed these bears for the Woodmans at a teddy bear event.* Courtesy of Robert and Pat Woodman. Photograph by Robert Woodman.

Illustration 177.
Robert Raikes Creations by Applause
Second Edition, Spring 1986. Limited edition of 15,000 of each design.

"For those who cherish America's heritage, Applause presents the second collection of Raikes Bears."

"The Raikes Originals are carefully detailed and sculpted to portray the life and style of the 1890s. This truly collectible series of fully-jointed bears features all new finely carved faces and detailed paw pads of light stained cypress.

"Each bear from this limited edition series is individually signed, numbered and comes boxed with its own certificate of authenticity and an ownership registration card.

"This edition of Raikes Originals expands the Raikes Bears family to thirteen. These bears are destined to become collector classics, like their older cousins.

"Very special creations from a very special artist."
(Raikes Collector Brochure, 1986.)
Note: A special edition of the second series of Raikes Bears was produced by Applause for the United Kingdom. Marked "UK Limited Edition," it appears there were 100 each of Max, Kitty *and* Arnold *and 230 each of* Benjamin, Christopher *and* Penelope.

The design and development of this new Avanti line dates back to 1980 when Larry Elins, President of Wallace Berrie, and Gary Trumbo, Vice President of Marketing, first noticed these beautifully-crafted animals at the Milan Toy Show. They were particularly impressed with the fine attention to detail, the quality construction and careful finishing. The animals had an unprecedented realism, from a natural sparkle in their eyes to the softness of their fur. It was almost as if the animals lived and breathed.

Upon inquiry, Elins and Trumbo learned that the animals, then marketed throughout Europe under the "Jockline" label, were created by Riccardo Chiavetta, formerly of the renowned plush manufacturing company, Aux Nations.

Wallace Berrie contacted Chiavetta and, through an arrangement with Jockline, acquired the worldwide marketing rights. Thus, the Avanti line began.

Applause does not rest on their past laurels. Merchandise ranges from plush animals to collectible figurines and stationery. Ceramics and home decor are also marketed and sold along with pencil huggers and mugs. A host of exciting new lines have recently been introduced: Dolls by Pauline, 101 Dalmations, Flavia Gift line and much more.

One new additional plush line will contribute profits to save endangered species of animals around the world. This new World Wildlife Fund features high quality plush designs that convey the true beauty of some of those creatures whose future may be in question. This licensed property was another example of Applause's commitment to quality toys.

Another extremely popular Applause line is that of the Raikes Bears. When bear artist Robert Raikes first approached Applause, they had never heard of a Raikes bear. Bob had sent them some photographs which peaked their interest in seeing what a Raikes bear looked like in person. When Applause finally met Bob and his bears, they realized that the Raikes bears were the most exciting and fresh product they had seen for quite awhile. There was no hesitation on their part to manufacture and market the Raikes bears.

Gary Trumbo presented a speech at the 1989 Robert Raikes Collector's Club First National Convention in Woodland Hills, California. Mr. Trumbo told the

Illustration 178. (Left) Kitty. Second Edition, Spring 1986. Raikes Bear by Applause. 24in (61cm) tall; brown acrylic fur; carved wooden face and foot pads; inset plastic eyes; jointed arms and legs; swivel head; signed and numbered on foot; limited edition of 15,000; style number 5458. "This high-stepping gal will steal your heart in her old-fashioned pink lace blouse and full moiré fabric Can-Can skirt." (Raikes Collector Brochure, 1986.)
(Right) Max. Second Edition, Spring 1986. Raikes Bear by Applause. 24in (61cm) tall; charcoal-colored acrylic fur; carved wooden face and foot pads; inset plastic eyes; jointed arms and legs; swivel head; signed and numbered on foot; limited edition of 15,000; style number 5460. "Better watch your cards. Max is a real ole-time card dealer sporting the traditional visor, black corduroy vest and garter." (Raikes Collector Brochure, 1986.) Courtesy of Robert and Carol Raikes.

BELOW: Illustration 180. Arnold. Second Edition, Spring 1986. Raikes Bear by Applause. 24in (61cm) tall; light gray acrylic fur; carved wooden face and foot pads; inset plastic eyes; jointed arms and legs; swivel head; signed and numbered on foot; limited edition of 15,000; style number 5459. "Arnold is ready to hit the greens in his dapper knickers, argyle sweater and velveteen tie, all topped off with a matching Scottish cap." (Raikes Collector Brochure, 1986.) Courtesy of Shirley Tish.

Illustration 179. (Left) Christopher. Second Edition, Spring 1986. Raikes Bear by Applause. 16in (41cm) tall; light brown acrylic fur; carved wooden face and foot pads; inset plastic eyes; jointed arms and legs; swivel head; signed and numbered on foot; limited edition of 15,000; style number 5455. "Off to the shore for a Sunday outing, Christopher's all decked out in a sailor's suit of red, white and blue complete with ribboned cap." (Raikes Collector Brochure, 1986.)

(Right) Penelope. Second Edition, Spring 1986. Raikes Bear by Applause. 16in (41cm) tall; beige acrylic fur; carved wooden face and foot pads; inset plastic eyes; jointed arms and legs; swivel head; signed and numbered on foot; limited edition of 15,000; style number 5457. "She's the life of the party and picture perfect in her pink party dress with lace detail and bow to match." (Raikes Collector Brochure, 1986.) Courtesy of Robert and Carol Raikes.

Illustration 182. Tyrone. *Second Edition, Spring 1986. Raikes Bear by Applause. 36in (91cm) tall; brown acrylic fur; carved wooden face and foot pads; inset plastic eyes; jointed arms and legs; stationary head; signed and numbered on foot; limited edition of 5000; style number 5461.* "All turned out in his black velvet and satin trimmed tux with pearl buttoned shirt. Tyrone will be the hit of the affair." *(Raikes Collector Brochure, 1986.)* Courtesy of Applause, Inc.

ABOVE: Illustration 181. Benjamin. *Second Edition, Spring 1986. Raikes Bear by Applause. 16in (41cm) tall; dark brown acrylic fur; carved wooden face and foot pads; inset plastic eyes; jointed arms and legs; swivel head; signed and numbered on foot; limited edition of 15,000; style number 5456.* "Ready for bed. Benjamin will sleep warm and toasty in his soft blue flannel back-flapped jammies and matching stocking cap." *(Raikes Collector Brochure, 1986.)* Courtesy of Robert and Pat Woodman. Photograph by Robert Woodman.

Illustration 183. Allison and Gregory, the Wedding Couple. *Summer 1986. Raikes Bears by Applause. 16in (41cm) tall; white acrylic fur; carved wooden face and foot pads; inset plastic eyes; jointed arms and legs; swivel head; signed and numbered on foot; limited edition numbered to 15,000 pairs; only 10,000 sets made; Allison — style number 5462.* Dressed in bridal gown and veil. Gregory — *style number 5462. Dressed in black velvet tuxedo, top hat, bow tie and white satin vest.*

Sold only as a pair in one collector box. One certificate per pair. Courtesy of Applause, Inc.

Illustration 184.
Robert Raikes Creations by Applause
Third Edition, Autumn 1986. Limited edition of 15,000 of each design.

"Applause Presents the Glamour Bears of the 1920s"

"From Lindberg's flight across the Atlantic, to the glamorous stars of the silver screen, new found independence, jubilant flappers with a zest for life, typify the events of the 'Roaring 20s.

"And now, Robert Raikes, the recognized artisan and sculptor, has masterfully captured in wood and plush as only he can, the personalities, characteristics and gaiety of the 20s era. Applause is proud to present this exclusive third edition of Robert Raikes Originals.

"Like all of Robert Raikes previous creations, these bears are fully-jointed and impeccably detailed, down to the embroidered 'Raikes Bears' name found on their clothing. This joyful series features new plush colors, and finely carved expressive faces and detailed paw pads all of lightly stained cypress.

"Individually signed and numbered, these limited editions of 15,000 each, come collector boxed with their own certificate of authenticity and ownership registration card."
(Raikes Collector Brochure, 1986.)

Illustration 185. *(Left)* Lindy. *Third Edition, Autumn 1986. Raikes Bear by Applause. 24in (61cm) tall; brown acrylic fur; carved wooden face and foot pads; inset plastic eyes; jointed arms and legs; swivel head; signed and numbered on foot; limited edition of 15,000; style number 5463.* "Ready for a tough flight across the Atlantic, Lindy's our leading man in his flight jacket, pilot's cap with goggles and World War I flying ace scarf." *(Raikes Collector Brochure, 1986.)* *(Center)* Daisy. *Third Edition, Autumn 1986. Raikes Bear by Applause. 16in (41cm) tall; variegated gray and black acrylic fur; carved wooden face and foot pads; inset plastic eyes; jointed arms and legs; swivel head; signed and numbered on foot; limited edition of 15,000; style number 5468.* "Daisy's right out of F. Scott Fitzgerald's Great Gatsby. A member of the 'smart set,' she's stylishly dressed in a gray pleated skirt, sweater and pink felt cloche." *(Raikes Collector Brochure, 1986.)* *(Right)* Reginald. *Third Edition, Autumn 1986. Raikes Bear by Applause. 16in (41cm) tall; variegated gray and black acrylic fur; carved wooden face and foot pads; inset plastic eyes; jointed arms and legs; swivel head; signed and numbered on foot; limited edition of 15,000; style number 5467.* "'Twenty-three skidoo!' In his felt beanie covered with popular slang buttons, argyle sweater, bow tie and class pennant our collegiate hero is ready to impress any girl he meets." *(Raikes Collector Brochure, 1986.)* Courtesy of Applause, Inc.

Illustration 186. *(Left) Cecil. Third Edition, Autumn 1986. Raikes Bear by Applause. 16in (41cm) tall; dark brown acrylic fur; carved wooden face and foot pads; inset plastic eyes; jointed arms and legs; swivel head; signed and numbered on foot; limited edition of 15,000; style number 5466. "Cecil's expression lets you know he's ready to shout 'Cut' but he's dressed for 'Action', complete with his director's megaphone, velvety red beret, monocle, satin ascot and khaki-colored safari jacket." (Raikes Collector Brochure, 1986.)*

(Center) Maude. Third Edition, Autumn 1986. Raikes Bear by Applause. 24in (61cm) tall; white acrylic fur; carved wooden face and foot pads; inset plastic eyes; jointed arms and legs; swivel head; signed and numbered on foot; limited edition of 15,000; style number 5464. "Maude has everything it takes to be a 'silent-movie' star. From her roaring '20s flapper dress in pink and aqua pastels with black satin trim to her long strand of pearls and perky felt cloche." (Raikes Collector Brochure, 1986.)

(Right) Zelda. Third Edition, Autumn 1986. Raikes Bear by Applause. 16in (41cm) tall; white acrylic fur; carved wooden face and foot pads; inset plastic eyes; jointed arms and legs; swivel head; signed and numbered on foot; limited edition of 15,000; style number 5465. "Zelda's ready to cut a rug in her black fringed frock and sequined headband. Her little pout tells you she's one bear who's not happy unless she's doing The Charleston." (Raikes Collector Brochure, 1986.)
Courtesy of Applause, Inc.

Illustration 187. Calvin *and* Rebecca. Rabbits. *Spring 1987. Raikes Rabbits by Applause. 18in (46cm) tall; carved wooden head and paws (jointed at ankles); painted eyes; unjointed cloth body.* Calvin — *style number 20137. Dressed in tweed pants and striped shirt.* Rebecca — *style number 20136. Dressed in floral dress with pinafore carrying a basket.*

First edition of rabbits. Unnumbered series. At this writing, 5000 of each have been produced. Calvin *and* Rebecca *were not manufactured with Robert Raikes' signature on the foot. Courtesy of Robert and Carol Raikes.*

Robert Raikes Creations by Applause
Fourth Edition, Spring 1987. Limited edition of 7500 of each design.

**Applause Presents the
"Americana Collection"**

Illustration 188. Miss Meloney. *"Americana Collection." Fourth Edition, Spring 1987. Raikes Bear by Applause. 24in (61cm) tall; brown acrylic fur; carved wooden face and paw pads; inset plastic eyes; jointed arms and legs; swivel head; signed and numbered on foot; limited edition of 7500; style number 17005. Dressed as a Southern Belle in a white and blue floral dress, white hat and blue tulle parasol.* Courtesy of Robert and Pat Woodman. Photograph by Robert Woodman.

BELOW: Illustration 189. Sara Anne. *"Americana Collection." Fourth Edition, Spring 1987. Raikes Bear by Applause. 16in (41cm) tall; cream-colored acrylic fur; carved wooden face and foot pads; inset plastic eyes; jointed arms and legs; swivel head; signed and numbered on foot; limited edition of 7500; style number 17002. Dressed in pink and white floral dress and hat.* Courtesy of Robert and Pat Woodman. Photograph by Robert Woodman.

Illustration 190. Margaret. *"Americana Collection." Fourth Edition, Spring 1987. Raikes Bear by Applause. 16in (41cm) tall; white acrylic fur; carved wooden face and foot pads; inset plastic eyes; jointed arms and legs; swivel head; signed and numbered on foot; limited edition of 7500; style number 17004. Dressed in a nurse's uniform.* Courtesy of Robert and Carol Raikes.

Illustration 191. Casey. *"Americana Collection." Fourth Edition, Spring 1987. Raikes Bear by Applause. 16in (41cm) tall; cream-colored acrylic fur; carved wooden face and foot pads; inset plastic eyes; jointed arms and legs; swivel head; signed and numbered on foot; limited edition of 7500; style number 17003. Dressed as a baseball player complete with baseball glove.* Courtesy of Robert and Carol Raikes.

collectors of the notable business, personal and humorous events he has shared with Bob since the beginning of what has proved to be a very successful working relationship.

Gary Trumbo spoke informally to the gathering.

He explained how Bob Raikes and Applause got together. It started with a Raikes letter and photos originally sent to Coleco. The packet found its way to Applause. A phone conversation ensued and when Applause discovered Bob's parents were showing his work in Los Angeles, they made arrangements to have Robert Raikes Sr. and his wife, Cathy, come to their head office in Woodland Hills on their way to the event and show their son's work to Gary Trumbo. Mr. Trumbo was so impressed, he purchased $2000 worth of Raikes' items.

He showed the creations to three focus groups — doll collectors, gift retailers and collector stores — and met with a fantastic reaction.

In Trumbo's talk, he went on to explain that after Bob and Carol and Applause came to a contract agreement, Applause sent samples to the Far East. There, too, he received assurance that the product could be made overseas.

He recalled Bob flying to the Orient in January 1985, and how customs officials questioned him at length about the tools he carried with him.

Trumbo and Raikes traveled to Taiwan and on to the southern tip called Tai-Chung, where Raikes sat on the floor teaching people to carve the now-famous wooden faces.

The rest of the week was devoted to making the outfits for the Raikes bears. The finished samples were hand-carried to New York. In Trumbo's words, "We knew we had a winner!"

Raikes was formally launched at the Los Angeles Gift Show (July 1985) with the media enthralled with Bob's carved samples. That first series, reported Trumbo, sold out in 30 days. Since that time, Applause has grown five-fold and Trumbo says (he likes to) think it was the (first) letter from Bob that helped. "Raikes is part of the wood work," he punned, alerting his audience to more mini-animals and upcoming limited edition musicals and Snowdomes.

Illustration 192. Andrew *and* Jill. *Spring 1988. Raikes rabbits by Applause. 23in (58cm) tall (including ears); dark brown acrylic fur; carved wooden face; velveteen foot pads and inner ears; painted eyes; unjointed arms and legs; stationary head; signed and numbered on foot; limited edition of 5000 each. (Left)* Andrew — *style number 20267. Dressed in blue and white striped vest with pink satin tie. (Right)* Jill — *style number 20266. Dressed in white, pink and blue floral dress.*
Second series of Raikes Rabbits. Courtesy of Robert and Carol Raikes.

Robert Raikes Creations by Applause
Beavers. Spring 1988. Limited edition of 5000 of each design.

Applause Presents the "Timber Creek Collection"

"Journey with us deep into the forest, far from the world of man. Peering through the trees, into a tiny clearing next to a gentle stream, we happen upon a bustling community of a different sort, The Beavers of Timber Creek.

"The Timber Creek Collection is the latest creation of the masterful artisan and sculptor, Robert Raikes, the creator of bears and rabbits. Through keen observation of his neighbors in the wilderness near his Mt. Shasta home, Robert Raikes captured the true nature of these unique and fascinating creatures, and interpreted them in his own inimitable style.

"The Beavers of Timber Creek are by nature busy little animals, yet we find them at a rare moment of leisure. Beaming at us with sweet, expressive faces, dressed in their best, each is a joyful reminder of the satisfaction which comes from a job well done.

"In limited editions of 5000, these new designs carry on the Raikes tradition of exquisitely detailed collectibles, finely crafted in delicately carved cypress and luxurious plush. And, of course, every piece in the collection is numbered and bears the signature of its creator.

"The Timber Creek Collection — an irresistible addition to the habitat you call home." (Raikes Collector Brochure, 1988.)
Illustration 193. Sam and Lucy. "Timber Creek Collection." Spring 1988. Raikes Beavers by Applause. 14in (36cm) tall; dark brown acrylic fur; dark brown velveteen tail;

carved wooden face, feet and paws; inset plastic eyes; jointed arms and legs; stationary head; signed and numbered on foot; limited edition of 5000 each. (Left) Sam — style number 17012. "Sam is wearing a sailor top, the same exquisite detailing as Lucy's. He also sports a white knit beret, which adds that special accent." (Raikes Collector Brochure, 1988.) (Right) Lucy — style number 17011. "Lucy is dressed for the country in a white sailor top beautifully detailed with navy blue ribbon edging and a red tie and a pleated skirt. Her big blue bow adds the finishing touch for a day in the country." (Raikes Collector Brochure, 1988.) Collector's tip. A percentage of Lucy's ties bore the name "Raikes Bears." Corrected ties read "Raikes Originals." Courtesy of Robert and Carol Raikes.

Robert Raikes Creations by Applause
Fifth Edition: Spring 1988. Limited Edition of 7500 of each design.

Applause Presents the "Sweet Sunday Collection"

"No one can resist the sweetness and innocence of a little toddler. And these little ones come straight from the nursery and into your heart.

"Capturing the very essence of a toddler's personality, the Sweet Sunday Collection is our newest Limited Edition of Raikes Bears.

"These bundles of joy are all dressed up in their Sunday Best and are, of course, on their best behavior.

"Only Robert Raikes, the masterful artisan and sculptor, could capture the softness of youth in the beautiful blend of wood and plush. These fully-jointed collectible bears are exquisitely detailed. From the satin ribbons in their hair to the eyelet petticoats to the embroidered designer name on their clothing.

"This lovable new collection captures the sweet rosy-cheeked innocence that adorns these baby's faces and sets them apart from the elder members of the Raikes family. Their lasting appeal is enhanced by the finely-carved and lightly-stained faces and paw pads.

"Individually signed and numbered, each Limited Edition of 7500 bears comes with its own collector box, Certificate of Authenticity, ownership registration card and this 5th Edition Raikes Collector Brochure.

"If you were lucky enough to acquire any or all of the first four editions of Raikes Bears, you already know that their market value has increased many fold since their introduction." (Raikes Collector Brochure, 1988.)

Illustration 194. *(Left)* Susie. *"Sweet Sunday Collection." Fifth Edition, Spring 1988. Raikes Bear by Applause. 16in (41cm) tall; light brown acrylic fur; carved wooden face and foot pads; inset plastic eyes; jointed arms and legs; swivel head; signed and numbered on foot; limited edition of 7500; style number 17008.* "I look forward all week to Sunday. That's when I put on my pretty pantaloons and dress up in my pink and blue flowered dress. The special one with the matching bonnet." (Raikes Collector Brochure, 1988.)
(Center) Sally. *"Sweet Sunday Collection."* *Fifth Edition, Spring 1988. Raikes Bear by Applause. 16in (41cm) tall; white acrylic fur; carved wooden face and foot pads; inset plastic eyes; jointed arms and legs; swivel head; signed and numbered on foot; limited edition of 7500; style number 17007.* "I love when mom puts the pink satin bow in my hair. Nobody can resist my charms when I toddle out in my pink cotton dress with the dainty flower pattern and applique trim." (Raikes Collector Brochure, 1988.)
(Right) Timmy. *"Sweet Sunday Collection." Fifth Edition, Spring 1988. Raikes Bear by Applause. 16in (41cm) tall; dark brown acrylic fur; carved wooden face and foot pads; inset plastic eyes; jointed arms and legs; swivel head; signed and numbered on foot; limited edition of 7500; style number 17009.* "Mom's always dressing me in 'her' favorite blue and white plaid playsuit with matching bow tie. At least the cotton weave feels light and comfortable to play around in." (Raikes Collector Brochure, 1988.)
Courtesy of Applause, Inc.

Illustration 195. Terry. Summer 1988. *Raikes Bear by Applause. 12in (31cm) tall; available in brown or white acrylic fur; carved wooden face and foot pads; inset plastic eyes; jointed arms and legs; swivel head; signed on foot; style number 17010.*

Unnumbered series. At this writing, 15,000 have been produced. Robert Raikes personally autographed these bears for the Woodmans at a teddy bear event. The Terry bear was also made in "black" acrylic fur (Center) as the Robert Raikes Collector's Club bear. Upon becoming a member, you receive one black Terry bear. (For more information on the Robert Raikes Collector's Club and the club bear, please refer to Chapter Six — The Robert Raikes Collector's Club.) Courtesy of Robert and Pat Woodman. Photograph by Robert Woodman.

Illustration 196.
Robert Raikes Creations by Applause
Sixth Edition, Summer 1988. Limited edition of 10,000 of each design.
Applause Presents the "Home Sweet Home Collection"
"Hot apple pie, cool glasses of lemonade, and Sunday dinner are just a taste of the warm and loving feelings of the Raikes Bears' Home Sweet Home Collection. Peek out the front window and see Emily, Jenny and Jason. These three siblings are the newest addition to the Raikes family. Charmingly crafted by the masterful artisan and sculptor, Robert Raikes, this collection will truly take you on a walk down memory lane with recollections of playtime on the porch, long talks on the swing, and warm breezes through the trees. Each bear beautifully depicts a "down-home" feeling, and their adorable faces are sure to touch your heart and conjure up reflections of your childhood." (Raikes Collector Brochure, 1988.)

Illustration 198. (Left) Jason. *"Home Sweet Home Collection." Sixth Edition, Summer 1988. Raikes Bear by Applause. 18in (46cm) tall; dark brown acrylic fur; carved wooden face and foot pads; inset plastic eyes; jointed arms and legs; swivel head; signed and numbered on foot; limited edition of 10,000; style number 17015. "Bespectacled Jason is irresistible with his button nose and charming waistcoat. His endearing face will tug at your heart strings and evoke a timeless feeling of the pleasant memories of bygone days. All three siblings will make you smile and tempt you to open up your 'Home Sweet Home' to their entire family." (Raikes Collector Brochure, 1988.)*
(Right) Jenny. *"Home Sweet Home Collection." Sixth Edition, Summer 1988. Raikes Bear by Applause. 18in (46cm) tall; brown acrylic fur; carved wooden face and foot pads; inset plastic eyes; jointed arms and legs; swivel head; signed and numbered on foot; limited edition of 10,000; style number 17014. "Jenny is a dainty little lady whose outfit is made of short heart print fabric edged with lace and accented with heart shaped buttons. Her petite night cap frames her adorable face with lace, reflecting the beautiful handcrafted design that has been demonstrated throughout all of Robert Raikes collections." (Raikes Collector Brochure, 1988.)* Courtesy of Robert and Carol Raikes.

Illustration 197. Emily. *"Home Sweet Home Collection." Sixth Edition, Summer 1988. Raikes Bear by Applause. 26in (66cm) tall; white acrylic fur; carved wooden face and foot pads; inset plastic eyes; jointed arms and legs; swivel head; signed and numbered on foot; limited edition of 10,000; style number 17013. "Emily, the eldest of the three siblings, is dressed in country charm with a flowered French blue dress and a pretty peach ruffled apron accented with a French blue satin ribbon. Her big blue bow adds a romantic touch to her precious outfit." (Raikes Collector Brochure, 1988.)* Courtesy of Robert and Carol Raikes.

LEFT: Illustration 199. Kevi. *Autumn 1988. Raikes Bear by Applause. 12in (31cm) tall; light brown acrylic fur; carved wooden face and foot pads; inset plastic eyes; unjointed arms and legs; stationary head; signed and numbered on foot; limited edition of 10,000; style number 17019.*

The concept for the Kevi bear came to Bob after he had met the internationally acclaimed singer and entertainer Kevin Roth. Bob was so impressed with the children's response to Kevin and his singing that Bob had the idea to make a bear with a tape recording ("Unbearable Bears") of Kevin's singing accompanying the bear. Courtesy of Robert and Pat Woodman. Photograph by Robert Woodman.

Illustration 200. *(Left) Mrs. Claus. Christmas 1988. Raikes Bear by Applause. 17in (43cm) tall; white acrylic fur; carved wooden face and foot pads; inset plastic eyes; jointed arms and legs; swivel head; signed and numbered on foot; limited edition of 7500; style number 21391. Dressed in wine-colored velvet dress with beige lace apron. (Right) Santa Claus. Christmas 1988. Raikes Bear by Applause. 17in (43cm) tall; white acrylic fur; carved wooden face, beard and foot pads; inset plastic eyes; jointed arms and legs; swivel head; signed and numbered on foot; limited edition of 7500; style number 21390. Dressed in wine-colored velvet Santa Claus outfit.*

First Christmas edition. Courtesy of Robert and Carol Raikes.

Illustration 201. *(Left)* Brett. *1989. Raikes Rabbit by Applause. 11in (28cm) tall; brown acrylic fur; light brown velveteen foot pads and inner ears; inset "blue" plastic eyes; unjointed arms and legs; stationary head; whiskers; signed on foot; style number 2041. Dressed in white pants and pink shirt.*
(Center Left) Ashley. *1989. Raikes Rabbit by Applause. 11in (28cm) tall; brown acrylic fur; light brown velveteen foot pads and inner ears; inset "blue" plastic eyes; unjointed arms and legs; stationary head; whiskers; signed on foot; style number 20400. Dressed in white and pink sun dress.*

Brett *and* Ashley *are an unnumbered series. At this writing, 15,000 of each have been produced. Note this is the first time Applause had used blue eyes on Robert Raikes animals.*
(Center Right) Mr. Nickleby. *Easter 1989. Raikes Rabbit by Applause. 16in (41cm) tall (ears not included); brown acrylic fur; light brown velveteen foot pads (sculptured) and inner ears; inset plastic eyes; jointed arms and legs; swivel head; whiskers; signed and numbered on foot; limited edition of 7500; style number 20399. Dressed in pink and white print dress and white hat.*

(Right) Mrs. Nickleby. *Easter 1989. Raikes Rabbit by Applause. 16in (41cm) tall; brown acrylic fur; light brown velveteen foot pads (sculptured) and inner ears; inset plastic eyes; jointed arms and legs; swivel head; whiskers; signed and numbered on foot; limited edition of 7500; style number 20398. Dressed in white shirt and slacks with a corduroy vest.*

Third edition of Raikes Rabbits. Courtesy of Applause, Inc.

Robert Raikes Creations
by The Good Company

Seventh Edition, Spring 1989. Limited edition of 10,000 of each design.

The Good Company Presents
the "Saturday Matinee Collection"

"Close your eyes and journey back to a simpler time. A time of jukeboxes, Saturday afternoon movies, bobby sox, and youthful innocence.

"It's the 50s and Robert Raikes, the masterful artisan and sculptor, has once again captured the spirit of the decade with his seventh edition, the Saturday Matinee Collection.

"Exquisitely detailed, these bears relive the playfulness of the 50s in an adorable blend of wood and plush, adorned by the costumes of their silver screen heroes.

"In keeping with Raikes' highest standards of excellence, these fully-jointed, finely crafted collectibles are in limited editions of 10,000 each. They come with their own Collector Box, Certificate of Authenticity and Ownership Registration Card. And, of course, each and every piece is numbered and bears the signature of its creator.

"Close your eyes...You can almost taste the popcorn, hear the thunder of hoofbeats and feel the 35¢ ticket stub in your hand...Now open them. It's the Raikes Saturday Matinee Collection." (Raikes Collector Brochure, 1989.)

Illustration 202. *(Left)* Lionel. *"Saturday Matinee Collection." Seventh Edition, Spring 1989. Raikes Bear by The Good Company. 24in (61cm) tall; brown acrylic fur; carved wooden face and foot pads; inset plastic eyes; jointed arms and legs; swivel head; signed and numbered on foot; limited edition of 10,000; style number 660281. "Lionel is the embodiment of Casey Jones himself in his engineer striped blue overalls and cap. Like any tyke following in the footsteps of his hero, he realizes the importance of accuracy and polishes off his look with a red bandana before 'headin' to the matinee." (Raikes Collector Brochure, 1989.)*

(Center) Bonnie. *"Saturday Matinee Collection." Seventh Edition, Spring 1989. Raikes Bear by The Good Company. 18in (46cm) tall; medium beige acrylic fur; carved wooden face and foot pads; inset plastic eyes; jointed arms and legs; swivel head; signed and numbered on foot; limited edition of 10,000; style number 660280. "Bonnie is the square dancer's favorite as she complements her hero, Jesse. In a darlin' blue denim skirt with white eyelet trim, red and white gingham blouse, and white cotton petticoat, she's ready for a Saturday afternoon with her best boy. She even has a matching 'cowgirl' hat!" (Raikes Collector Brochure, 1989.)*

(Right) Jesse. *"Saturday Matinee Collection." Seventh Edition, Spring 1989. Raikes Bear by The Good Company. 18in (46cm) tall; light beige acrylic fur; carved wooden face and foot pads; inset plastic eyes; jointed arms and legs; swivel head; signed and numbered on foot; limited edition of 10,000; style number 660279. "Yee-Haw! Jesse is rootin'-tootin' ready for his favorite Matinee in his blue denim jeans and red flannel shirt. His little white vest with Sheriff's star, cowboy hat, and red bandana neckerchief could even bring a smile to anyone's face!" (Raikes Collector Brochure, 1989.)*

It appears the style numbers on the bears do not coincide with the Raikes Collector Brochure. The style numbers on the bear are as follows: Jesse #17021, Bonnie #17022, Lionel #17023. In addition, the size of Lionel in the Raikes Collector Brochure is 24in (61cm) and the bear measures 18in (46cm). Courtesy of The Good Company.

Illustration 203. *(Left) Lionel. "Saturday Matinee Collection." Seventh Edition, Spring 1989. Raikes Bear by The Good Company. 18in (46cm) tall.*
(Right) Lionel (Artist Proof). "Saturday Matinee Collection." Seventh Edition, Spring 1989. Raikes Bear by The Good Company. 18in (46cm) tall.
Note the distinctive difference between the two bears. The Artist Proof's hat is sewn on the left, the "Raikes Bears" stitching (plural). "AP" precedes number on foot, production tag sewn on back reads "Product of Taiwan ROC," not "Made in the Philippines." Applause "Artist Proofs" are models given to Production to create the Originals. There are generally 350 of each model made. They are not for sale but sometimes slip through into the retailers' market. They are a rarity and in some cases more valuable than the Originals themselves. An interesting article about Lionel was published in the Fall 1989 issue of Bearrister Bugle:

"Out of the 10,000-piece production run, a small number of rare Lionels which are distinctively different from the majority, were released to the general public.

"In February of 1989, Applause/Good introduced the 'Saturday Matinee Collec- tion,' the seventh edition of Raikes Bears by that company. This set, made up of Jesse the Cowboy, Bonnie the Cowgirl, and Lionel the Train Engineer, had a limited production run of 10,000 pieces each.

"According to Joe Dumbacher, a produc- tion manager at Applause/Good in Wood- land Hills, California, 390 of the Lionels produced were made in Taiwan rather than the Philippines, where the rest of the 'Satur- day Matinee Collection' pieces were manu- factured.

"These 'Taiwan Lionels' are distin- guished from the majority as follows: The hat is perched on his left rather than on his right; the number on the foot is preceded by "AP"; the production tag is located at his upper back rather than near the tail and reads 'Product of Taiwan, ROC' rather than 'Made in the Philippines;' and the stitching on his overalls reads 'Raikes Bears' (plural); (The debate as to whether 'Raikes Bear,' which is stitched on all other Saturday Matinee pieces, was a deviation from the registered trademark and thus itself a production error is another story.)

"Why 'AP,' for Artist Proof, was stamped on these 390 Lionels is not clear. A true Artist Proof Lionel, noted by AP on the foot with no number, was auctioned off by Robert Raikes at the October 1988 Bristol, Connect- icut bear show. Happily, that true artist proof was purchased by a fellow Raikes-collecting couple.

"One more point, Taiwan Lionels are not simply Lionels 1 through 390. For exam- ple, number 320/10,000 is not a Taiwan piece. Thus, these 'AP' bears are not consecu- tively numbered." Courtesy of Robert and Pat Woodman. Photograph by Robert Woodman.

OPPOSITE PAGE: Illustration 204. *An- nie. "Mother's Day Collection." 1989. Raikes Bear by The Good Company. 16in (41cm) tall; white acrylic fur; carved wooden face and foot pads; inset plastic eyes; jointed arms and legs; swivel head; signed and num- bered on foot; limited edition of 7500; style number 660283. Dressed in pink and white dress.* Courtesy of The Good Company.

Illustration 205. Cookie. *Spring 1989. Raikes Bears by The Good Company. 12in (31cm) tall; available in brown or gray acrylic fur; carved wooden face and foot pads; inset plastic eyes; jointed arms and legs; swivel head; signed on foot.*

Unnumbered series. At this writing, 30,000 have been produced. Robert Raikes personally autographed these bears for the Woodmans at a teddy bear event. Courtesy of Robert and Pat Woodman. Photograph by Robert Woodman.

Illustration 206 *(Left)* Juliette. *Spring 1989. Raikes doll by The Good Company. 14in (36cm) tall; carved wooden head and arms; painted blue eyes; unjointed cloth body; signed and numbered on back; edition of 7500; style number 660285. Dressed in christening outfit.*

Comes in a basket. First edition of Raikes dolls. This design was reproduced from Robert Raikes original one-of-a-kind baby doll (Illustration 67).

(Right) Molly. *Spring 1989. Raikes doll by The Good Company. 16in (41cm) tall; carved wooden head, arms and legs; painted brown eyes; unjointed cloth body; black hair; signed on back of doll in black ink "A Robert Raikes;" comes with stand; signed and numbered on stand; limited edition of 7500; style number 660284. Dressed in pink gingham dress.*

Molly *and* Juliette *are the first edition of Raikes dolls. The design for* Molly *was taken from Robert Raikes original* Molly *doll (Illustration 68). Courtesy of The Good Company.*

RIGHT: Illustration 207. (*Left*) Maid Marion, the Hedgehog. *"Sherwood Forest Collection." Spring 1989. Raikes Hedgehog by The Good Company. 20in (51cm) tall; variegated dark brown acrylic fur; carved wooden face, paws and feet; inset plastic eyes; jointed arms and legs; swivel head; signed and numbered on foot; limited edition of 7500; style number 660332. Dressed in gold, beige and pink satin dress and burgundy and pink cape.*
(*Right*) Robinhood Raccoon. *"Sherwood Forest Collection." Spring 1989. Raikes Raccoon by The Good Company. 16in (41cm) tall; variegated brown acrylic fur; carved wooden face, paws and feet; inset plastic eyes; jointed arms and legs; swivel head; signed and numbered on foot; limited edition of 7500; style number 660331. Dressed as Robin Hood.* Courtesy of The Good Company.

Illustration 209. Liza. *Summer 1989. Raikes Bear by The Good Company. 13in (33cm) tall; white acrylic fur; carved wooden face and foot pads; inset plastic blue eyes; unjointed arms and legs; stationary head; signed and numbered on foot; edition of 10,000; style number 660376. Dressed in pink and white dress.*

A tape recording ("The Secret Journey Bear Lovin") of world famous singer and entertainer Kevin Roth accompanies the bear. Note this is the first Robert Raikes Bear produced by Applause and The Good Company with blue eyes. Courtesy of The Good Company.

LEFT: Illustration 208. (*Top Row*) Santa. *Christmas 1989. Raikes Bear by The Good Company. 14in (36cm) tall; white acrylic fur; carved wooden face, beard and foot pads; inset plastic eyes; jointed arms and legs; swivel head; signed and numbered on foot; limited edition of 7500; style number 660334. Dressed in Santa Claus outfit.*

Second edition of a Santa Claus. The sack is for display purposes only.
(*Bottom Row*) Elves. *Christmas 1989. Raikes Bears by The Good Company. 12in (31cm) tall; white acrylic fur; carved wooden face and foot pads; inset plastic eyes; jointed arms and legs; swivel head; signed on foot; unnumbered series. At this writing, 20,000 have been produced; style number 660335. Available in red or green corduroy elf outfits.*

The style of the outfits appears to vary slightly within edition. Courtesy of The Good Company.

Robert Raikes Creations by Applause
The Three Bears. Autumn 1989. Limited edition of 7500.

"They're No Fairy Tale"

"Once upon a time, a brilliant sculptor named Robert Raikes, introduced the world to a remarkable band of bears. In a few short years, the Raikes Bears have become known and loved throughout the world and are now one of the most prized collectibles in existence.

"The Good Company is proud to be associated with Mr. Raikes and is very privileged to announce that a whole new Bear family is about to emerge from the woods. Meet The Three Bears: Papa, Mama and Baby.

"You'll lose your heart the first time you see these captivating creatures. Each one is a fine example of the outstanding quality and incredible attention to detail that have always been the hallmark of Raikes Bears.

"This furry family is so lifelike that you'll swear they're whispering together every time you turn your back. Probably wondering if you're related to that little girl who caused them so much trouble.

"You'd better reserve a set right away because these are destined to be rare bears indeed. Only 7,500 signed and numbered sets will be produced so it would be easy to miss out.

"Of course, the good news is, that even when you're just eating porridge, relaxing in an easy chair or snuggled safely in bed, these Raikes Bears will be increasing in value. Year after year.

"That's no fairy tale. That's for real. Because, like a good fairy tale, a Raikes Bear only gets better as time goes by." (**Teddy Bear & friends**®, *December 1989*).

Illustration 210. *The Three Bears. Autumn 1989. Raikes Bears by The Good Company.*
(Left) Father Bear. *12in (31cm) tall; short dark brown acrylic fur; carved wooden face, paws and feet; inset plastic eyes; unjointed arms and legs; stationary head; signed and numbered on foot. Dressed in brown tweed trousers, cream-colored shirt with bow tie.*
(Center) Baby Bear. *7.5in (18cm) tall; short dark brown acrylic fur; carved wooden face, paws and feet; inset plastic eyes; unjointed arms and legs; stationary head; signed and numbered on foot.*

(Right) Mother Bear. *12in (31cm) tall; short light brown acrylic fur; carved wooden face, paws and feet; inset plastic eyes; unjointed arms and legs; stationary head; signed and numbered on foot. Dressed in brown skirt, cream-colored blouse, pink apron and cap.*

The Three Bears *are mounted on a wooden base. Style number for all three bears is 661434. A limited edition of 7500 sets. Courtesy of The Good Company.*

Eighth Edition, Spring 1990. Limited edition of 7500 of each design.

"Summer Fun at Camp Grizzly..."

"*Relive the nostalgic memories of your first summer camp — the tangy scent of pine trees, the clean mountain air, the warmth of a campfire and the crispy sweetness of roasted marshmallows.*

"*In this, his eighth edition, the masterful artisan and sculptor, Robert Raikes, has captured the fun, excitement and woes of a child's first camping expedition with the 'Camp Grizzly' trio of characters dressed in authentic camping gear.*

"*The Camp Grizzly Collection continues the Raikes tradition of collectibility with a theme that has special appeal to children and adults alike. Each of Robert Raikes' creations increases in value over the years and the Camp Grizzly Collection promises to be no exception. These fully-jointed, finely crafted collectibles are in limited editions of 7,500 pieces each. They come with their own Collector Box, Certificate of Authenticity and Ownership Registration Card. And, of course, each and every piece is numbered, with the signature of its creator.*" (Raikes Collector Brochure, 1990.)

Illustration 211. Hillary. *"Camp Grizzly Collection." Eighth Edition, Autumn 1989. Raikes Bear by The Good Company. 16in (41cm) tall; dark cinnamon-colored acrylic fur; carved wooden face and foot pads; inset plastic eyes; jointed arms and legs; swivel head; signed and numbered on foot; limited edition of 7500; style number 661431.* "With her cheerful face and bright orange windbreaker, Hillary portrays all the eagerness and exuberance of a young girl on her first adventure." (Raikes Collector Brochure, 1990.) Courtesy of The Good Company.

ABOVE: Illustration 213. Jeremy. *"Camp Grizzly Collection." Eighth Edition, Autumn 1989. Raikes Bears by The Good Company. 16in (41cm) tall; dark cinnamon-colored acrylic fur; carved wooden face and foot pads; inset plastic eyes; jointed arms and legs; swivel head; signed and numbered on foot; limited edition of 7500; style number 661432.* "Ruggedly attired in cap, vest, shorts, and orange scarf, Jeremy tugs at the heart. With his pouting expression, he reflects the trepidation that accompanies the unknown." (Raikes Collector Brochure, 1990.) Courtesy of The Good Company

RIGHT: Illustration 212. Wendell. *"Camp Grizzly Collection." Eighth Edition, Autumn 1989. Raikes Bears by The Good Company. 24in (61cm) tall; dark brown acrylic fur; carved wooden face and foot pads; inset plastic eyes; jointed arms and legs; swivel head; signed and numbered on foot; limited edition of 7500; style number 661430.* "Wendell is the Camp Master, inspiring memories of camp leaders who protected us from the perils of the great outdoors. From his Smokey the Bear hat to his backpack, suspenders, and whistle, Wendell is the spitting image of authority." (Raikes Collector Brochure, 1990.) Courtesy of The Good Company.

With our company, they can be sold to true collectors and be represented by a company with a reputation for collectibility.

It is an interesting study to follow a Raikes prototype from start to an Applause finished product:

1. First, the prototype is sent to the Orient with instructions concerning the clothing and type of plush to be used.

2. Then, the Applause vendor makes a duplicate sample which is sent to Robert Raikes for approval.

3. At that point, Bob approves or disapproves the duplicate sample. Applause makes any necessary corrections at its overseas manufacturers.

4. In the meantime, Applause starts working with the Art Department on a look for the Collector Box, Official Certificate of Authenticity, the Ownership Registration Card and the Raikes Collector Brochure. The brochure is colorfully illustrated with valuable information regarding the artist and the animals. (Noted in the illustration captions are the products that include the Raikes Collector Brochure.)

5. The artwork is sent to Bob for his approval.

6. An identification hang-tag is attached to each animal's arm. In addition is the company's production label sewn into the back seam.

7. The limited editions are hand-numbered on the foot and the majority of all the products display the signature of Robert Raikes.

8. The product is produced.

9. The wood Applause uses for the Raikes bears is cypress, maple or white wood.

10. Robert Raikes approves all the names of the bears, but some of them have a cute history. For instance, *Sara Ann*, *Ashley* and *Eric* are named after Applause executives' relatives. *Emily*, *Jenny* and *Jason* were named after Robert Raikes' children. *Andrew* and *Jill Bunny* were named after an Associate Product Manager (and her husband) who was working with Raikes.

So, at Applause, even a fantasy bear like a Raikes bear has a logical step-by-step birthing process prior to becoming a child's toy or a collector's treasure.

Illustration 215. *Each limited edition of Raikes creations by Applause is hand-numbered (example: X2254/7500 is piece number 2254 out of 7500) and displays the signature of Robert Raikes. The unnumbered series just displays Robert Raikes' signature. With the exception of* Jamie, Sherwood, Calvin *and* Rebecca, *their feet were blank (no signature or number).* Courtesy of Robert and Pat Woodman. Photograph by Robert Woodman.

Illustration 214. Sophie. *Valentine Bear. Winter 1990. Raikes Bear by The Good Company. 12in (31cm) tall; white acrylic fur; carved wooden face and foot pads; inset plastic eyes; jointed arms and legs; swivel head; signed on foot; style number 661380. Wearing white ruffle with pink ribbon around neck; pink ribbon bow at ear.*

Note foot pads carved in the shape of a heart. Unnumbered series. Courtesy of The Good Company.

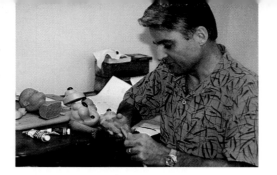

Illustration 217. Bob, working on a prototype for Applause in his studio.

Chapter Four

The Creation of a Robert Raikes Teddy Bear

Robert Raikes has been called the "modern day Gepetto," after the famed creator of Pinocchio. He loves to carve and approaches each piece of wood as if it were a new adventure. His imagination, hard work and attention to detail have earned him the reputation of being one of America's most successful and admired teddy bear artists today.

Being involved in the world of teddy bears for so many years myself, I appreciate how collectors thirst for information about their hobby. I have found the more learned about the area in which one collects, the more interesting the hobby becomes.

So I asked Bob to share with us how he creates his famous Raikes teddy bears.

"When I first get an inspiration for a new design, I go to my drawing board and quickly make a rough sketch. By working fast, I let my feelings really flow onto the paper. There is no need for fine detail at this point, as I feel it slows down your creativity. I make progressive drawings. For example, on one page I will sketch the first design of a bear, then I'll draw the same sketch, only this time maybe give the bear a tongue, then onto the next sketch changing the dimensions somewhat (*Illustration 216*).

"After I feel satisfied with the final sketch, I draw half of the profile of my final design onto a piece of tracing paper. To be sure the face is symmetrical, I fold the paper in half, so now when I begin working with the clay, my background is perfectly matched. Placing a ball of clay onto my drawing, I draw a line down the center of the clay for a guide. Not paying too much attention to the drawing at this point, I begin the creative process of working on the face. Once I get the basic look and proportions, I compare the picture with the clay and decide which I like better.

"Once the main design is completed, I make my hard copy in wood. After finely sanding, any necessary corrections are made. Then, I recarve some parts and do the final detail work. The eyes are glued in place, and the features are then carefully painted. Finally, I apply a clear protective coat.

"For each carved wooden prototype I make for Applause, I also make a resin copy from the original clay sculpture. In some cases it may be necessary to grind or add resin to the copy until I am completely satisfied with the design. The resin copy gives the exact proportions and allows Applause to put the hard copy on their machine. The wooden prototype gives the coloration. I complete and dress the body so Applause can see exactly how the finished product should look.

"Sometimes, the Applause prototype goes back and forth between me and Applause before I give my final approval. I must be satisfied with the Applause version of my work and that it represents my original.

"This procedure can take up to six months before the piece is finally ready for production. Applause normally likes to have my designs at least one year in advance. However, I am now working several years ahead with my designs. Mentally, I'm five years ahead."

Bob concluded our interview by saying laughingly, "I only hope my work continues to sell as well as it is now so I may use all these ideas I have."

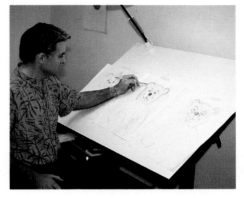

Illustration 216. When Robert Raikes first gets an inspiration for a new design, he goes to his drawing board and quickly makes a rough sketch. Here he is seen making these first progressive drawings.

Chapter Five

Illustration 219. *Young Kerianne Mills (age five) was overjoyed to have Robert Raikes personally sign her* Sherwood *at my San Diego Teddy Bear, Doll and Antique Toy Festival in 1988. Robert Raikes autographed over 1600 of his bears that day.* Courtesy of Georgann Mills.

Robert Raikes' Philosophy of Life

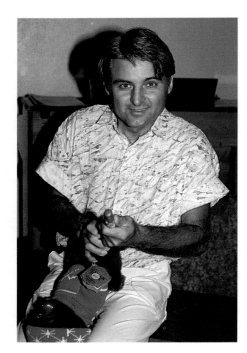

Illustration 218. *When I first invited Robert Raikes to autograph his creations at my San Diego Teddy Bear, Doll and Antique Toy Festival in 1986, the talented artist "hand-carved" his signature on the foot of hundreds of his bears manufactured by Applause.*

From the very first time I met Robert Raikes at a doll show at the Anaheim Convention Center in California in 1982, he gave me the feeling of a person who not only cared about his work, but sincerely cared about people.

Busy as he was the day of the show, surrounded by collectors wanting to buy his wonderful creations, he would take time to talk to each individual, letting them know that everyone of them was very special to him, and he was sincerely interested in their questions and remarks.

Basically, Robert Raikes is a very shy, soft-spoken person. His father recalls how nervous his son was when talking to people about his work. "I really had to persuade Bob to do shows, as he was really shy," explained Mr. Raikes Sr. "He would always stand in the background and watch. When collectors would ask who the artist was, I would point to my son and say, 'there he is,' and young Bob would immediately take off."

I appreciated Bob's talent as a sculptor from the time I saw his work. Bob and Carol exhibited their own work when I produced my first Teddy Bear and Antique Toy Festival in San Diego, California, in 1983. I feel very proud to have had them as a part of this very special event in my life.

After Bob and Carol entered into the contract with the gift company of Applause, I witnessed incredible reactions to the Raikes bears. I had the idea to invite the popular artist and his wife, Carol, to be guests at my 1986 San Diego Teddy Bear and Antique Toy Festival. I proposed he would autograph his bears by Applause and demonstrate his carving talents. As this would be Bob's first signing at a show, it took quite a lot of persuasion on my part before the shy artist consented. I anticipated a good response at the show from Bob and Carol's appearance, but my estimation was far below the crowds of collectors that stood in line for hours with their arms full of bears.

One lady appeared with a baby buggy overflowing with Raikes bears. Many collectors' cars were jammed full of bears to be signed. One of the most amazing things to me about those early signings was that Bob actually hand-carved his name on the foot of each bear. Bob carved his name on over 1500 bears that day (*Illustration 218*). He signed from 10 a.m. to 4 p.m. with no break, even for lunch. I asked him, "How can you even hold a carving tool for that long?" He smiled saying, "I can carve my name almost as fast as I can write with a pen."

I have been very fortunate to have Bob appear at my San Diego festivals for four years to date. With each signing, hundreds more men, women and children of all ages appear at the show, unable to resist the appeal of the Raikes bears. They are now avid collectors. However, it is not just the bears that have won the hearts of collectors, but the artist himself. His warm, caring attitude has brought him almost as much fame as his bears. Bob lets people know they are important to him and they return this feeling. I have watched Bob at shows patiently listening to collectors endless questions, stories and looking at numerous pictures of their Raikes bear collections.

When I began research for this book, Bob and his wife, Carol, kindly invited my husband and me to spend a weekend with them at their house in Mount Shasta, California. This enabled me to not only photograph Bob's original work, but to interview the couple in the relaxed atmosphere of their home.

It was a beautiful, crystal clear fall day when we arrived. The smell of the giant California pine trees was so refreshing, I could easily see why Bob would get his inspirations by living in this tranquil, natural mountain setting. The weekend I spent at the Raikes' home was not only lots of fun, but a very memorable and inspiring experience.

We got up early in the morning, as we planned to photograph Bob's original work in the pristine, verdant setting of Mount Shasta. I gazed out of the window just in time to see Bob taking off for his early morning bike ride (*Illustration 220*).

BELOW LEFT:Illustration 220. One of Bob's favorite pastimes is his early morning bike ride. This daily event in his life is not only one of his favorites, but he says it clears his mind and gives him time to prepare for his full day ahead in his studio.

This daily event in Bob's life is not only one of his favorites, but he said it clears his mind and gives him time to prepare for his full day ahead in his studio.

We all had so much fun that day photographing the bears. With the enthusiasm and the excitement of young children, we all romped through the woods, finding the ideal spot to photograph Bob's wonderful bears and animals. We even risked our lives climbing the huge mountain rocks and jumping over the fast flowing rivers to get that ideal picture (*Illustration 221*). That evening, tired but happy and pleased with the achievements of the day, we sat in the cozy den of Bob and Carol's home. I was not only warmed by the huge, crackling fire, but the warmth shared by the Raikes family. Their two daughters, Jenny (ten) and Emily (eight), were extremely interested in my authoring a book about their father's work and their family.

Bob expressed the importance of letting his children feel their involvement. "When we were making the dolls and bears, before they went anywhere, they had to be inspected by the children." Bob admits Jenny and Emily were their strongest critics. "They thought that all the dolls and bears were theirs. I think they must believe they live in Santa's house. The dolls and bears are an integral part of our lives. Our children are always around our work and for them it's normal to have bears and dolls all over our dining room and kitchen tables."

It is an everyday sight to see the children sitting watching television with the bears and dolls all around them. A precious sight the evening we were there was that of young Emily, curled up into the arms of Bob's huge 5ft (152cm) original

ABOVE: Illustration 221. Bob and I had so much fun photographing the bears in beautiful areas surrounding his Mount Shasta home. With the enthusiasm and excitement of young children, we romped through the woods and even risked our lives climbing the huge mountain rocks and jumping over fast flowing rivers to get that ideal picture.

Illustration 223. *Jenny was delighted when her father created a set of bears named after his children. Here Jenny happily shows off the finished products of* Jenny *(left) and* Jason *(right).* Courtesy of Robert and Carol Raikes.

bear (*Illustration 222*). "Ever since she was a little girl, this has been one of her favorite places to sit at night," Bob said.

I found Carol to be everything everyone told me about her — sweet, reserved, soft-spoken and a devoted wife and mother. She was reluctant to discuss her invaluable contribution to Bob's career. She never mentioned how hard she worked and the loyal support she had given her husband during those long hard years, but instead, focused on the good times and their plans for the future. Since signing the contract with Applause, Carol no longer has to help Bob with his work. Therefore, she devotes all her time to her family.

Bob and Carol shared so much of their life with me that weekend. It was Bob's philosophy of life that impressed me the most. He told of the hard times and how much he and Carol had sacrificed to reach the point where they were today. He said it was a growing period for them and they were both stronger and learned so much from those experiences. "When I was young," Bob recalls, "like most young men my age, I wanted to change the world. Actually, I'm still trying to do it. I know I can't change it, but I do plan to make a lot of people happy. I think the whole reason I got into art in the first place was not only to do creative work and do something special with my life, but I wanted to show people I cared about them. We live in a society that is much too fast. There is very little caring out there. My first and most important goal with my work is to try and bring a little joy into the world. I have a basic Christian philosophy of caring for others, and I sincerely try to put that feeling in my work. People really do come first with me. Carol and I have had to go without a lot for over a decade. If I had wanted to cut corners and not show I cared through my work, I could have made it in different ways with my artwork. But, I wasn't willing to do that."

Bob's voice was firm but very sincere as he told me this. "It's only amusing in retrospect, but we have lost many a night's sleep when we were making our dolls and bears. We'd driven long distances in one day to do a show, getting up at three o'clock in the morning and not getting back until eleven o'clock at night.

Illustration 222. *A precious sight the evening I visited the Raikes home was that of Bob's young daughter, Emily, curled up into the arms of Bob's huge 5ft (152cm) original bear.*

Illustration 225. Robert Raikes Sr. and his wife, Cathy, opened up their home and their hearts to me during my 1988 visit. They allowed me to photograph their whole collection and answered endless questions regarding their son's work.

Illustration 224. Cathy and Robert Raikes Sr.

We did this to avoid paying for a motel which, fortunately, we do not have to worry about as much anymore."

I asked Bob what advice he could give to the artists just beginning. "Just put all your heart and energy into your work." He went on to say how he feels he wasted a lot of years going in different directions. "Try to be systematic and professional. I wish I had learned more about the business world in the beginning. You need to have people around you that are both encouraging and critical and help you with your work. If you believe in yourself and know where you're going, you can make it. It is so rewarding for me to know there are approximately 80,000 of my products out there, sitting on shelves throughout the world making people smile on a daily basis. It's so easy to make people happy," said Bob smiling. "If I can make people happy with just a teddy bear, think what people can do with a lot more talent and insight than me. I had no formal art training. My success comes from a God-given gift, an inner peace and an insight that I feel helps me put joy in my work."

On the return journey home from my memorable weekend in Mount Shasta with Bob Raikes and his family, I had the pleasure of visiting the home of Bob's parents, Robert Raikes Sr. and his wife, Cathy. They lived in the beautiful coastal town of Los Osos, California. I was overwhelmed when I walked into their home with their collection of Bob's original work. It was virtually a Robert Raikes museum.

Cathy smiled and explained how several of the pieces in their collection were discarded prototypes that did not satisfy their son. She went on to tell me how she had managed to rescue them before the salvage truck came and these rare pieces of her son's work would have been gone forever.

It was soon apparent the sculptor's warm and sensitive personality was part of his heritage. Mr. Raikes Sr. and his wife were truly two of the most genuine, wonderful people I have ever met.

Their faces beamed with pride as they related events in their son's successful career.

I was delighted to find they had saved several of the very first dolls and teddy bears Bob created, and many additional examples of his early carvings. What originally was only to be an afternoon at Bob's parents house turned into two full days.

Robert Raikes Sr. and Cathy opened up their home and their hearts to me, allowing me to photograph their whole collection (*Illustration 225*) and answering my endless questions regarding their son's work.

Chapter Six

The Robert Raikes Collector's Club

For a long time Bob had been receiving hundreds of letters from collectors requesting the formation of a Robert Raikes Collector's Club. The need for information regarding the Raikes products and up-to-date news on Bob's appearances and special events was evident from the number of requests.

Bob knew to do a good job, it would entail a lot of time and work, both of which his busy life style did not really allow. However, after serious consideration and with the valuable help of his secretary, Marilyn Santos, Bob formed the Robert Raikes Collector's Club in June 1988.

The collectors' response to the club was overwhelming. After only six months, more than 1000 members had enrolled and to date there are over 5500 members.

An informative newsletter, *Bear Facts*, is also published quarterly, and is available through the club for an annual subscription of $5.00.

Bob's goal was to make the club special and truly fun. He designed an attractive membership invitation. Colorfully decorating the cover is talented artist Steve Oerding's rendition of a Raikes bear mailing his membership in a mailbox while Mama and baby bear watch from the front of their Victorian home (*Illustration 227*). Inside the invitation are pictures of Bob at various events and working in his studio.

In addition is a letter to the collectors from Bob:

"Dear Collectors,

"Hello, to all of you who have given good homes to the bears & dolls that I have created. My hope is, they are bringing you lots of joy and happy smiles. It's my pleasure to give you a personal invitation to join the RRCC, and all the fun and excitement that goes along with membership.

"We have monthly drawings for originals that you can only win if you are a member. To date we have given away thousands of dollars in originals.

"We have a computer you can call for all sorts of fun information and contests. We also have an extra special newsletter that is available with great

Illustration 226. *Bob and his secretary, Marilyn, are continually working on new ideas for the Robert Raikes Collector's Club.*

Illustration 227. *Talented artist Steve Oerding colorfully decorated the cover of the Robert Raikes Collector's Club membership invitation with his rendition of a Raikes bear mailing his membership in a mailbox.* Courtesy of Steve Oerding.

Terry. Robert Raikes Collector's Club Bear. 1988. Raikes Bear by Applause. 12in (31cm) tall; black acrylic fur; carved wooden face and foot pads; inset plastic eyes; jointed arms and legs; swivel head; signed and numbered on foot; style number 17010.

Terry *was produced in black for the Robert Raikes Collector's Club bear. It is given to the members of the Raikes club upon becoming a member.*

stories and information including a list of people throughout the country buying and selling Raikes' creations.

"I am constantly planning new and exciting things for club members, not to mention very special limited editions for club members and club member stores.

"$5.00 a year gives you a great newsletter. This is your club and we want your participation.

"My pledge is to put the same care into the RRCC as goes into the designing of each of my little friends.

"Sincerely,

"Robert Raikes"

At this writing there have been two competitions whereby a club member has a chance to win one of Bob's original pieces.

The first was the "Dress a Raikes Bear" contest. The rules were to use an undressed Raikes bear. For example: *Sherwood, Jamie, Terry* or the club bear (*Terry*, made in black acrylic fur) and design an original outfit for the bear. The contestants were given from January 1, 1989, to April 30, 1989, to mail in a picture of their entry. On May 1, 1989, Bob chose a winner. Over 100 entries were received.

"It was a difficult decision for Bob as there were so many creative outfits," stated Marilyn. She went on to say, "After much consideration, Bob decided that awarding one prize just wouldn't do. So he picked five winners. First place went to Pat Woodman (*Illustration 229*). Bob sent her an original white rabbit (*Illustration 230*). Other winners received cash prizes and Raikes memorabilia."

The second competition was a giant "Coast-to-Coast Teddy Bear Hunt." The object of this hunt was to find the stores across the United States to which Bob had given the clues. The first member to gather all the clues was the winner of a Raikes original.

The hunt commenced on September 1, 1989, and the collectors were all given the following clues:

#1 You can find your first shop in Des Moines, Iowa.

#2 First word of clue: "Raikes," find your next clue in Anaheim, California.

#3 Second word of clue: "Bears," find your next clue in New Cumberland, Pennsylvania.

#4 Third word of clue: "Are," find your next clue in Miami, Florida.

#5 Fourth word of clue: "#1," find your next clue in Estes Park, Colorado.

#6 Fifth word of clue: "Phone home, with all pieces of clue."

The winner of the competition was club member Lael Luise Berkstresser. Lael amazed everyone when she found all the clues in three hours.

Illustration 229. Pat Woodman won first place in the Robert Raikes Collector's Club "Dress a Bear" contest in 1989 when she dressed her Terry *bear, 12in (31cm) in this regal-looking outfit of taffeta and velvet. It took Pat three weeks from designing the outfit to the completion. Pat named her creation the "Fairy Bear." (For further information on the* Terry *bear, see Illustration 195). Courtesy of Robert and Pat Woodman. Photograph by Robert Woodman.*

When I phoned Lael to ask her about the "Coast-to-Coast Teddy Bear Hunt," she was happy to share with me a detailed account of how she tracked down all the clues:

"On September 1, 1989, I called the Raikes Collector's Club computer newsline first thing in the morning. I had called several times the day before in case the new recording was up as I hoped to find that an original was for sale. Listening to the recording, I found that two originals were available to the first ones calling at 9 a.m. I also learned about the 'Giant Teddy Bear Hunt.'

"The first clue was to be found in Des Moines, Iowa. I went to my binder with all my Raikes Collector's Club information and quickly found that Bob had a signing at Reflections in Des Moines last May. At my inquiry, the lady at Reflections said, "Your clue is 'Raikes' and your next clue will be found in Anaheim, California."

"At 10 a.m. I called the Bear Tree (where I had often visited and where I knew Bob had a signing last November), and got my second clue ...."Bears" and the next clue would be found in New Cumberland, Pennsylvania. Another easy one.... Looking at my list, I quickly called Bears and Wares. They gave me my third clue, "Are" and told me the next clue was in Miami, Florida.

"Miami, Florida. Nothing on my list. A very early newsletter mentioned Miami but no store. I made numerous phone calls and spoke with some great people. I explained what I was doing and asked for names of stores where they had purchased the bears they had. Several were club members and knew of the hunt, although only one was also trying to find all the clues. Most had not purchased any in Miami proper; I was referred to stores in surrounding communities. Each store that I called, I asked for referrals to other stores in the area. Finally, as I called one last ad from *Collectors United*, the gentleman who answered gave me several stores, none of which were in Miami; a lady in the background mentioned Cindy's Florist. He told me that Cindy's Florist was in Miami but he didn't think that would help. I told him that I appreciated any help and that if they weren't participating, they might know other stores in the same distributorship.

"I called Cindy's Florist and explained what I was doing. The minute I mentioned Raikes' Giant Teddy Bear Hunt, the gentleman responded: your clue is "#1" and the next clue is Estes Park, Colorado!

Illustration 231. Eric Schwartz was the lucky winner of the January 1989 Robert Raikes Collector's Club drawing. Courtesy of Eric Schwartz.

Illustration 230. The first prize of the Robert Raikes Collector's Club "Dress a Bear" contest was a magnificent Robert Raikes original one-of-a-kind rabbit. Pat Woodman was the lucky winner with her entry in Illustration 229. *Rabbit is a Robert Raikes original. 16in (41cm) tall; white acrylic fur; hand-carved wooden face; white Ultrasuede foot pads and inner ears; inset plastic eyes; jointed arms and legs; swivel head; hand-signed on foot "Robert Raikes 1989."* Courtesy of Robert and Pat Woodman. Photograph by Robert Woodman.

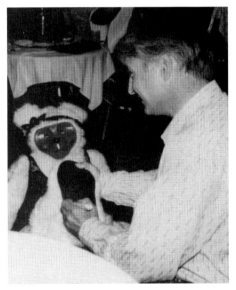

Illustration 232. The winner of the "Costume Contest" held at the first Robert Raikes Collector's Club Convention was Jan Mitzel. Jan's magnificent costume depicting a Raikes' Zelda bear (right) is truly a work of art. Jan's husband, Dan, also entered the competition dressed as Cecil (left). Dan artistically created the faces in papier-mâché and Jan made the fur costume. Courtesy of Dan and Jan Mitzel.

Illustration 233. An amusing sight at the Raikes convention was Robert Raikes autographing the foot of Jan Mitzel's costume. Courtesy of Dan and Jan Mitzel.

"While searching for Miami and looking for ads in the *Teddy Bear and friends*® magazine, I noticed an ad for a store in Estes Park....It stood out because I am active in credit unions and Estes Park is where the credit union act was signed. I immediately went back to my magazine and found the ad for *The Talking Teddy*. I called and a wonderful excited lady told me "You're our first caller." She then told me, 'Your clue is — phone home with all the clues.' I thanked her and immediately called Marilyn with all the clues, stores, cities and states. It was almost noon and I was so thrilled."

When Bob's secretary, Marilyn, told him the news of the winner of the hunt and how quickly all the clues were found, Bob responded by saying, "I can see I will have to make it a little harder next time."

However, Bob felt Lael's performance was worth a very special prize. So he awarded her a 38in (97cm) original *Tyrone* (worth approximately $2500 at that time — today's value $4500). An extra surprise for Lael was when Marilyn drove all the way to meet her in Hayward, California, and personally delivered the magnificent prize.

An additional attraction for club members are the monthly drawings. Here again members have a chance to win an original piece of Bob's work.

The prize for the January 1989 drawing was an original *Kevi* bear, and the lucky winner was eleven-year-old Eric Schwartz (*Illustration 231*). Eric is an avid Raikes bear collector and a strong admirer of Robert Raikes.

When Eric's class was given a school project to research a notable person, many of his classmates chose famous people from their history books such as Abraham Lincoln, Albert Einstein, Dwight Eisenhower and William Shakespeare, but Eric chose to research the life of Robert Raikes.

The newsletter also prints many of the club members' questions with Bob's or Marilyn's answers. For example, in the June 1989 issue of *Bear Facts*, Marilyn answered the question "How do you care for your Raikes animals?" "I have found by personal experiences that the best coverup for scratches on the wood is a walnut. I smash the nut between my fingers and work the oil and nut into the scratch. It may take a few minutes to soak in, then wipe off the excess nut meat to a nice finish. The fur is not washable, but if you have a spot, you might try a damp cloth and gently rub the spot. If your critters have been taking dust baths, then you might try the vacuum, but not on full power. Reduce the suction if you can, or you may wind up with (bare) animals. I've never heard of this happening but there's a first time for everything. Keep your animals out of direct sun; it fades the fur. clothing and makes a mess of the wood finish. Bob is always hesitant to tell you what to put on the wood for fear of an accident. Please be careful with anything you put on the wood. If you purchased a new piece of quality furniture and asked them what to use on the wood, chances are they would suggest one of the fruit oils. You might try this on the wood, but please keep it off the fur. A little goes a long way."

A very special event in the life of Robert Raikes that involved the club was the "First Robert Raikes Collector's Club Convention," held in Woodland Hills, California, October 13 through 15, 1989. ABC Unlimited Productions was contracted by Bob to coordinate the weekend's activities. The convention was open to club members only and proved to be a huge success. The theme for the event was "Pirates of the Pacific." In honor of the convention, Bob designed a special limited edition of bears (2500 pairs), *Billy Buccaneer* and *M'Lady Honeypot* (*Illustration 234*).

A special treat for the conventioneers was a tour of Applause, in Woodland Hills, California. Bob gave a wood-carving demonstration, and then everyone was invited to try their talents to a hands-on workshop. Under the supervision of the celebrity carver himself, the students completed their own versions of a Raikes bear face.

The guest speaker at the banquet was Applause Vice-President, Gary Trumbo. Gary entertained the gathering by recalling the notable, business, personal and humorous events he had shared with the successful sculptor.

Applause Product Manager, Joe Dumbacher, gave an informative slide presentation on Raikes creations produced by Applause. Robert Woodman, avid Raikes collector and historian, gave a magnificent slide presentation of his collection of Bob's original work.

One of the highlights of the event was the "Costume Contest." Entrants were asked to "Dress Like Your Favorite Raikes Bear or Pirate." "The response and hard work that went into the costumes was overwhelming," said Bob, recalling the event.

The winner of the female "Dress Like Your Favorite Raikes Bear" category was Jan Mitzel. Jan's husband, Dan, made the head of papier-mâché and Jan made the fur costume (*Illustration 232*). The winner of the male "Dress Like A Raikes Pirate" was Nick Herring.

"It was an extremely hard decision for the jury," said Bob, "as there were some magnificent costumes."

The convention was such a huge success that plans for the next convention began immediately.

Illustration 234. (Left) M'Lady Honeypot. *"Pirates of the Pacific" series. Summer 1989. Raikes Bears by The Good Company. 12in (31cm) tall; dark brown acrylic fur; carved wooden face and foot pads; inset plastic eyes; jointed arms and legs; swivel head; signed and numbered on foot; style number 30178. Dressed in black skirt and hat and gold satin blouse.*

(Right) Billy Buccaneer. *"Pirates of the Pacific" Collection. Autumn 1989. Raikes Bears by The Good Company. 12in (31cm) tall; dark brown acrylic fur; carved wooden face, foot pad and peg leg; inset plastic eyes; jointed arms and legs; swivel head; signed and numbered on foot; style number 30178. Dressed as a pirate in a black velvet coat, colorful bandana and a black patch over one eye.*

Sold as a pair. Limited edition of 2500. Robert Raikes designed the "Pirates of the Pacific" edition in celebration of the First Robert Raikes Collector's Club Convention in 1989. Courtesy of Robert and Pat Woodman. Photograph by Robert Woodman.

ABOVE: Illustration 235. Raikes Snow-domes: *Exciting new first edition Raikes musical snowdomes, 5¹/₂in (14cm), are highly detailed replicas of some of the most beloved and popular designs of Robert Raikes. There's Penelope ("The Sound of Music"), Eric ("Let It Snow"), Benjamin ("Brahms Lullaby"), Susie, Timmy and Sally ("My Favorite Things"), and Tyrone and Kitty* ("The Anniversary Waltz"). *Dedicated collectors will want them all. Suggested retail: $22.50.*

BELOW: Illustration 236. *Raikes mini figures - Tyrone (tuxedo), Casey (baseball), Rebecca (red dress) and Annie (pink and white dress), 2¹/₂in (6cm) high. June 1991 introduction, 2nd Edition.*

LEFT: Illustration 237. Brian & Sport/ Stacie & Fifi: *These carefree country Raikes Bears, 16in (41cm), come with furry little friends. Brian, with his puppy, and Stacie, with her kitten. Bears are fully jointed, and are available in limited editions of 10,000. Each Raikes Bear is signed and numbered on the right paw, and includes a certificate of authenticity and registration card. Dedicated collectors will love this tenth edition from Robert Raikes. Suggested retail: $120 each.*

Illustration 238. *Raikes mini figures -* Lindy *and* Chelsea, *2½in (6cm) high. February 1991 introduction, 1st Edition.*

LEFT: Illustration 239. *Raikes dolls -* Claire *(blonde) and* Abigail *(brunette), 17in (43cm) tall, June 1991 introduction.*

A Chronology of Robert Raikes

1947 — Born October 13, in Van Nuys, California.
Son of Robert and Cathy Raikes.

1968 to 1970 — Served in the United States Navy.

1970 — August 15, married Carol Morris.

1970 — Began wood sculpting after being inspired by Gilbert Valencia, chief carver for the Weatherby Rifle Company.

1973 to 1976 — Attended California Polytechnical College.

1973 to 1978 — Lived in Morro Bay.

1974 — Joined the National Carvers' Association.

1974 — May 23, first child, Jason, was born.

1974 to 1976 — Taught carving at Adult Education classes and at several high schools.

1974 to 1976 — Continued wood carving as a full-time profession, sculpting from mantels and headboards to figures and animals.

1975 — Created the first dolls, under the name of "Little Wooden Children."

1978 — Moved to Grass Valley, California.

1978 — October 9, second child, Jenny, was born.

1980 — Moved to Mt. Shasta, California.

1980 — April 19, Emily was born.

1981 — Won award in the "Fly Away" contest for best novice carver.

1981 — Commissioned to carve two life-size carousel horses by Holiday Inn in Santa Margarita, California.

1981 — Exhibited at first doll show in Santa Rosa, California.

1981 to 1983 — Concentrated on making dolls.

1982 — Began creating teddy bears under the name of *Woody Bear*.

1982 — Doll becomes more sophisticated. With the introduction of the dolls with all hand-carved wooden bodies, Bob changed the name of his creations to "Raikes Originals."

1984 — October, unable to meet the increasing demand for his products, Bob signed a contract with the well-known gift company Applause to produce his creations. In the agreement, Bob was still able to produce special order bears under the name *Woody Bear*.

1987 — October 13, Bob's 40th birthday, the artist made the decision that a good portion of his original work will be produced especially for special events, competitions, various charities and the Robert Raikes Collector's Club.

1988 — May, The Good Company becomes a division of Applause, Inc.

1988 — June, the Robert Raikes Collector's Club is formed.

1988 — December 6-11, appeared as a celebrity guest at the First Annual Walt Disney World Teddy Bear Convention in Florida.

1989 — October 13-15, the First National Convention of the Robert Raikes Collector's Club held in Woodland Hills, California.

1989 — November 28 - December 6, appeared as a celebrity guest at the Walt Disney World's Showcase of Dolls and Second Annual Teddy Bear Convention in Florida.

1989 — December 7, Applause and The Good Company consolidate, creating one full-line gift company - Applause, Inc.

The costumes for the majority of the different size bears appear to have been introduced in the following sequence.

Boys 24in (61cm) tall Tuxedo
 Vest and Tie
 Overalls
 Train Engineer
 Swiss-style Outfit

Girls 24in (61cm) tall Country-style Dress
 Ballerina
 Swiss-style Dress

Girl 18in (46cm) tall Ballerina
 Party Dress

Boy 18in (46cm) tall. Knitted scarf and hat. Came in dark blue and white with the name "Woody Bear" knitted into the scarf in white.
 14in (36cm) tall No clothes
 10in (25cm) tall No clothes

Tyrone 38in (96cm) Majority dressed in tuxedos; a small percentage were dressed as a Scotsman or in a Hawaiian shirt.

Girl 24in (61cm) tall Dress and Pinafore
 Dress, Pinafore and Bonnet

Boy 18in (46cm) tall Vest and Tie
 Wool Pants, Shirt and Ribbon Bow Tie

Girl 18in (46cm) tall Party Dress
 Swiss Dress and Bonnet
 Nightgown and Mop Cap

Robert Raikes Bear & Doll Price Guide

by
Linda Mullins

Copyright 1991 Linda Mullins

Introduction

Collecting Robert Raikes creations is increasing in popularity every year. The large number of collectors entering this field inspired me to write the price guide.

Robert Raikes has been creating his original dolls since 1975 and his bears since 1982, and these pieces have appreciated considerably.

But in 1984, when Robert Raikes was unable to meet the increasing demand for his products, he signed a contract with the major gift and licensing company, Applause, Inc., to produce his creations. By Applause, Inc. producing limited editions, this still kept Raikes' work highly select, but enabled many more collectors the opportunity to purchase his work. Applause does not solely produce limited editions, but does control the flow of Raikes' products, keeping them relatively valuable.

The Applause bears designed by Robert Raikes were an instant success. The impact they made on the collector's market was unbelievable. They appreciated in price at an outstanding rate.

The prices in this guide have been determined by studying shows, auctions, printed advertising, prices in newspapers and magazines. By examining the current market as well as price trends over the last year, I have done my very utmost to bring you the most up-to-date prices to the best of my ability.

Prices on Raikes "originals" are not included when not enough have been sold to establish a consistent price/value on the piece.

However, the current values in this booklet should only be used as a guide. The establishment of value must be yours in the end.

Prices may vary due to dealer philosophy and even the fancy of a collector. For instance, an informed and well-invested collector may choose to pay much more than book value for a piece because it completes a set. Or it may be that a collector attends an auction and simply dearly covets a particular piece. So those and similar situations cannot be taken into account when regarding the average bear.

Similarly, this guide is not meant to set prices from one section of the country to another. For instance, California prices for Raikes' work appear to be the highest.

Since prices are greatly influenced by condition as well as demand, please note that prices given in this guide are for pieces in excellent condition or, in the case of Raikes creations produced by Applause or The Good Company, the price would include the original collector box and certificate.

In various instances, the animals and dolls in the illustrations referred to in the price guide will have been personally autographed by Robert Raikes. However, the prices given in the guide are for pieces not personally autographed by Robert Raikes.

Neither the author nor the publisher assumes responsibility for any losses which may occur as a result of issuing this guide.

Whether you are an experienced or novice collector of Robert Raikes' work, I hope this price guide will aid you when considering purchasing or selling his bears and/or dolls.

Collecting Robert Raikes creations is a fun and exciting hobby, but if you wish to become more knowledgeable and deepen your understanding of his remarkable work, it requires a lot of study and self-education.

With this price guide (coupled with my book *The Raikes Bear & Doll Story*), your hobby will hopefully become ultimately more satisfying and rewarding.

Robert Raikes Creations By Applause
Price Guide

Illustration Number	Original Retail Price	1991 Price Guide	Name	Style Number	Size
			First Edition: Autumn 1985 7500 Pieces Each		
172	$100	$ 695-up	Rebecca	#5447	22in (56cm)
172	$100	$ 295-up	Sebastian	#5445	22in (56cm)
173	$ 65	$ 275-up	Bentley	#5448	14in (36cm)
173	$ 65	$1000-up	Chelsea	#5451	14in (36cm)
173	$ 65	$ 595-up	Eric	#5449	14in (36cm)
174	$100	$ 275-up	Huckle Bear	#5446	22in (56cm)
			Autumn 1985 Unnumbered Pieces		
175	$ 20	$ 80-up	Jamie (Brown and Gray)	#5453	10in (25cm)
176	$ 35	$ 125-up	Sherwood (Light Brown and Dark Brown)	#5452	13in (33cm)
			Second Edition: Spring 1986 15,000 Pieces Each		
178	$100	$ 225-up	Kitty	#5458	24in (61cm)
178	$100	$ 225-up	Max	#5460	24in (61cm)
179	$ 65	$ 350-up	Christopher	#5455	16in (41cm)
179	$ 65	$ 575-up	Penelope	#5457	16in (41cm)
180	$100	$ 225-up	Arnold	#5459	24in (61cm)
181	$ 65	$ 350-up	Benjamin	#5456	16in (41cm)
182	$300	$ 625-up	Tyrone*	#5461	36in (91cm)

* Only 5000 pieces

Illustration Number	Original Retail Price	1991 Price Guide	Name	Style Number	Size
			Wedding Couple Summer 1986 10,000 Pairs		
183	$150/pair	$ 550/pair	Gregory**	#5462	16in (41cm)
183			Allison**	#5462	16in (41cm)

** Numbered to 15,000 pairs
   Only 10,000 pairs made

Illustration Number	Original Retail Price	1991 Price Guide	Name	Style Number	Size
			Third Edition: Glamour Bears of the 1920s Autumn 1986 15,000 Pieces Each		
185	$100	$ 695-up	Lindy	#5463	24in (61cm)
185	$ 65	$ 200-up	Reginald	#5467	16in (41cm)
185	$ 65	$ 195-up	Daisy	#5468	16in (41cm)
186	$100	$ 200-up	Maude	#5464	24in (61cm)
186	$ 65	$ 495-up	Zelda	#5465	16in (41cm)
186	$ 65	$ 175-up	Cecil	#5466	16in (41cm)
			First Edition: Rabbits Spring 1987 Unnumbered Pieces		
187	$ 75	$ 425-up	Rebecca*	#20136	18in (46cm)
187	$ 75	$ 425-up	Calvin**	#20137	18in (46cm)

 * Rebecca: Total of 5000 pieces produced to date
** Calvin: Total of 5000 pieces produced to date

Illustration Number	Original Retail Price	1991 Price Guide	Name	Style Number	Size
			Fourth Edition: Americana Collection Spring 1987 7500 Pieces Each		
188	$100	$ 150-up	Miss Melony	#17005	24in (61cm)
189	$ 65	$ 150-up	Sara Anne	#17002	16in (41cm)
190	$ 65	$ 225-up	Margaret	#17004	16in (41cm)
191	$ 65	$ 250-up	Casey	#17003	16in (41cm)
			Second Edition: Rabbits Spring 1988 5000 Pieces Each		
192	$ 75	$ 200-up	Jill	#20266	23in (58cm)
192	$ 75	$ 200-up	Andrew	#20267	23in (58cm)
			Timber Creek Collection (Beavers) Spring 1988 5000 Pieces Each		
193	$ 75	$ 100-up	Sam	#17012	14in (36cm)
193	$ 75	$ 100-up	Lucy	#17011	14in (36cm)
			Fifth Edition: Sweet Sunday Collection Spring 1988 7500 Pieces Each		
194	$ 75	$ 200-up	Sally	#17007	16in (41cm)
194	$ 75	$ 200-up	Susie	#17008	16in (41cm)
194	$ 75	$ 150-up	Timmy	#17009	16in (41cm)
			Summer 1988 Unnumbered Pieces		
195	$ 28	$ 45-up	Terry (White and Brown)	#17010	12in (31cm)

Total of 15,000 pieces produced to date

Illustration Number	Original Retail Price	1991 Price Guide	Name	Style Number	Size
		Sixth Edition: Home Sweet Home Collection Summer 1988 10,000 Pieces Each			
197	$125	$ 140-up	Emily	#17013	26in (66cm)
198	$ 80	$ 125-up	Jason	#17015	18in (46cm)
198	$ 80	$ 150-up	Jenny	#17014	18in (46cm)
		Autumn 1988 10,000 Pieces			
199	$ 75	$ 90-up	Kevi	#17019	12in (31cm)
(Comes with Kevin Roth Tape)					
		Christmas 1988 7500 Pieces Each			
200	$100	$ 200-up	Santa	#21390	17in (43cm)
200	$100	$ 200-up	Mrs. Claus	#21391	17in (43cm)
		Third Edition: Rabbits Easter 1989 7500 Pieces Each			
201	$ 85	$ 125-up	Mr. Nickleby	#20399	16in (41cm)
201	$ 85	$ 125-up	Mrs. Nickleby	#20398	16in (41cm)
		Rabbits Easter 1989 Unnumbered Pieces			
201	$ 30	$ 60-up	Ashley	#20400	11in (28cm)
201	$ 30	$ 60-up	Brett	#20401	11in (28cm)
Total of 15,000 pieces produced to date					

Robert Raikes Creations By The Good Company

Illustration Number	Original Retail Price	1991 Price Guide	Name	Style Number	Size
		Seventh Edition: Saturday Matinee Collection Spring 1989 10,000 Pieces Each			
202	$ 75	$ 145-up	Lionel	#17023	18in (46cm)
202	$ 75	$ 125-up	Bonnie	#17022	18in (46cm)
202	$ 75	$ 125-up	Jesse	#17021	18in (46cm)
		First Edition: Mother's Day 1989 7500 Pieces			
204	$ 80	$ 225-up	Annie	#660283	16in (41cm)
		Spring 1989 Unnumbered Pieces			
205	$ 28	$ 35-up	Cookie Bear (Gray and Brown)	#660330	12in (31cm)
Total of 30,000 pieces produced to date					
		First Edition Dolls: Spring 1989 7500 Pieces Each			
206	$125	$ 125-up	Molly	#660284	16in (41cm)
206	$150	$ 150-up	Juliette	#660285	14in (36cm)
		Sherwood Forest Collection: Spring 1989 7500 Pieces Each			
207	$ 95	$ 110-up	Robinhood Raccoon	#660331	16in (41cm)
207	$ 95	$ 110-up	Maid Marion the Hedgehog	#660332	20in (51cm)
		Summer 1989 10,000 Pieces			
209	$ 90	$ 110	Liza	#660376	13in (33cm)
(With Kevin Roth Tape)					
		First Edition: Robert Raikes Collector's Club Convention Pirates of the Pacific Autumn 1989 2500 Sets			
234	$200/set	$ 400-up/pair	M'Lady Honeypot	#30178	12in (31cm)
234			Billy Buccaneer	#30178	12in (31cm)
		Christmas 1989 7500 Pieces			
208	$100	$ 175-up	Santa	#660334	14in (36cm)
		Christmas 1989 Unnumbered Series			
208	$ 40	$ 70-up	Elves (Green, Red)	#660335	12in (31cm)

Illustration Number	Original Retail Price		Name	Style Number	Size
		Three Bears on Wooden Base Autumn 1989 7500 Sets			
210	$220	$ 240-up/set	Three Bears	#661434	12in (31cm)
		Fourth Edition: Rabbits Spring 1990 7500 Pieces Each			
	$ 85		Aunt Mary Lou	#661416	12in (31cm)
	$ 85		Uncle Vincent	#661427	12in (31cm)
	$ 40		Betsy Ann	#661428	8in (20cm)
	$ 40		Vincent, Jr.	#661429	8in (20cm)
		Eighth Edition: Camp Grizzly Collection Spring 1990 7500 Pieces Each			
211	$ 90		Hillary	#661431	16in (41cm)
212	$130		Wendall	#661430	24in (61cm)
213	$ 90		Jeremy	#661432	16in (41cm)
		First Edition: Valentine's Day Spring 1990 Unnumbered Pieces			
214	$ 40		Sophie	#661380	12in (31cm)
		Second Edition: Mother's Day 1990 7500 Pieces Each			
	$135/set		Charlotte	#661433	11in (28cm)
			Toby	#661433	6in (15cm)
		Spring 1990 10,000 Pieces			
	$ 85		Courtney	#662027	12in (31cm)
		Nursery Miniatures Spring 1990 10,000+ Pieces Each			
	$ 36		Lisa Marie	#38518	7in (18cm)
	$ 36		Nathan	#38519	7in (18cm)
	$ 36		Ben	#38520	7in (18cm)
	$ 36		Allison	#38521	7in (18cm)
	$ 36		Robbie	#38522	7in (18cm)
	$ 36		Mitzi	#38523	7in (18cm)
		Ninth Edition: The Royal Court Autumn 1990 10,000 Pieces Each			
	$180		King William	#662347	22in (56cm)
	$180		Queen Mary	#662348	22in (56cm)
	$110		Court Jester	#662349	14in (36cm)
		Second Edition: Robert Raikes Collector's Club Convention Autumn 1990 1500 Pieces			
	$175		Calico Pete	#30304	13in (33cm)
		Christmas 1990 10,000 Pieces			
	$110		Classic Santa	#662031	12in (31cm)
		Snowdomes Christmas 1990 10,000 Pieces Each			
235	$ 45		Tyrone & Kitty	#38510	5-1/2in (14cm)
235	$ 45		Sally, Susie & Timmy	#38512	5-1/2in (14cm)
235	$ 45		Eric	#38513	5-1/2in (14cm)
235	$ 45		Penelope	#38514	5-1/2in (14cm)
		Walt Disney World Convention Christmas 1990 500 Pieces			
	$195		Dolly & Rocking Horse	#40259	8in (20cm)
		Fifth Edition: Rabbits Spring 1991			
	$180/pair		Mrs. Hopkins*	#53048	10in (25cm)
			Mr. Hopkins*	#53048	10in (25cm)
	$ 36		Cabria**	#53049	8½in (21cm)
	$ 36		Daniel**	#53050	8½in (21cm)

  * The Hopkins: Limited Edition 10,000 pieces each
 ** Cabria and Daniel: Unnumbered pieces

Illustration Number	Original Retail Price	Name	Style Number	Size
		Second Edition: Valentine's Day July 1991 1800 Pieces		
	$ 50	Cupid Bear	#662265	11in (28cm)
		Tenth Edition: Best Friends Collection Spring 1991 10,000 Pieces		
237	$120	Brian	#38516	16in (41cm)
		Sport	#38516	4-1/2in (5cm)
237	$120	Stacie	#38517	16in (41cm)
		Fifi	#38517	4-1/2in (5cm)

Robert Raikes Original Bears & Dolls
Price Guide

Illustration Number	Name	Year	Description	Size	1991 Price Guide
DOLLS					
37	Pouty-face Boy Doll	1975	cloth body, carved wooden hair	27in (69cm)	$3500-up
43	Girl Doll	1981	cloth body, synthetic hair, "big eyed" series	25in (64cm)	$3000-up
49	Clown Doll	1982	cloth body	22in (56cm)	$3800-up
53	(Left) Boy Doll	1982	cloth body, hand-carved hair	23in (58cm)	$3500-up
	(Right) Girl Doll	1982	cloth body, synthetic hair	22in (56cm)	$3000-up
60	Jester Doll	1984	all hand-carved wood, articulated head and body, brown feathers for hair	18in (46cm)	$4000-up
63	Girl Doll	1984	all hand-carved wood, articulated head and body, synthetic hair	26in (66cm)	$4500-up
BEARS					
91	Woody Bear	1983	burned wood effect	18in (46cm)	$3000-up
				24in (61cm)	$3500-up
92	Sherwood. Woody Bear	1983		14in (36cm)	$1200-up
93	Jamie. Woody Bear	1984		9.5in (23cm)	$950-up
100	Woody Bear	1984		20in (51cm)	$3000-up
108	Masque Face Ballerina. Woody Bear	1984		18in (46cm)	$3500-up
122	Panda. Woody Bear	1986		24in (61cm)	$4500-up
124	Baby Bear. Woody Bear	1986		16in (41cm)	$2000-up
125	(Left) Chelsea-face Woody Bear	1986		18in (46cm)	$2000-up
	(Middle Left) Pouty-face Ballerina Woody Bear	1985		18in (46cm)	$1900-up
	(Middle Right) Sailor. Woody Bear	1985		18in (46cm)	$1900-up
	(Right) Pouty-face Woody Bear	1986		18in (46cm)	$1900-up
126	(Left) Swiss Girl. Woody Bear	1986		23in (58cm)	$3000-up
	(Center) Ballerina. Woody Bear	1987		23in (58cm)	$3000-up
	(Right) Country Girl. Woody Bear	1986		23.5in (60cm)	$3000-up
127	Tyrone. Woody Bear	1986	Dressed as a Scotsman	38in (97cm)	$4500-up
130	(Left) Train Engineer. Woody Bear	1987		22in (56cm)	$3000-up
	(Center) Country Boy. Woody Bear	1986		23in (58cm)	$3000-up
	(Right) Swiss Boy. Woody Bear	1986		23in (58cm)	$3000-up
134	Kevi. Woody Bear	1987		14in (36cm)	$2000-up
135	Joey. Woody Bear	1987		12in (31cm)	$1000-up
140	(Left) Emily. Woody Bear	1988		24in (61cm)	$3000-up
	(Center) Jason. Woody Bear	1988		18in (46cm)	$1700-up
	(Right) Jenny. Woody Bear	1988		18in (46cm)	$1800-up
MISCELLANEOUS					
149	Rabbit (prototype)	1986		21in (53cm)	$2500-up
150	Rabbits	1986		23in (58cm)	$3800-up/ pair
152	Bunny	1987		8.5in (22cm)	$750-up
156	(Left) Hedgehog	1987		15in (38cm)	$1300-up
	(Center) Beaver	1987		16in (41cm)	$1200-up
	(Right) Owl	1987		12in (31cm)	$1000-up
157	Monkey	1987		23in (58cm)	$2000-up
158	Pigs	1987		23in (58cm)	$3500-up/ pair
159	Cat	1989		20in (51cm)	$1200-up

INDEX

朗朗中文
Yes! Chinese

Chinese Curriculum for Young Learner - Textbook 2B

海外少儿中文课程 — 第2B册

国家汉办/孔子学院总部 | YCT二级适用教材
Hanban/Confucius Institute Headquarters | **Curriculum for YCT Level-2**

姓名：
NAME _____

班级：
CLASS _____

www.yes-chinese.com

Welcome to Yes! Chinese, the most effective Chinese learning experience by Yes! Chinese.

Langlang Chinese is a complete Chinese Language learning curriculum for young students. It integrates comprehensive in-class instruction with interactive home studies. The Langlang Chinese adheres to the Hanban Youth Leaner Chinese Test (YCT) standard.

Langlang Chinese engages students with interactive online animated courses and highly intuitive textbooks. It fully utilizes the latest education technologies to offer a content-rich Chinese language learning experience for both classroom and home environments.

Books One and Two of the Chinese Starter book set are the first stages of the Langlang Chinese program. Available in various formats, they develop students' listening and speaking skills via multimedia lessons themed around daily activities. The level of difficulty of Book One is equivalent to level one as defined in the YTC, and Book Two is equivalent to level two as defined in the YCT.

The Chinese Starter book set includes both a text-book and a work-book. Supplementary materials include flashcards, interactive CDs, and online courses. We also provide a detailed teaching guide for teachers.

The development of the Langlang Chinese program was a collaborative effort between Chinese language scholars, experienced teachers, and enthusiastic parents across the English-speaking world. The material is easy to teach, fun to learn, and one of the most effective courses available today.

Please enjoy.
Executive Editing Committee
Yes! Chinese Creative Language Education Center

《朗朗中文》水平等级对应表
Yes! Chinese VS. YCT / HSK Testing Level

《朗朗中文》 Langlang Chinese	汉语水平 YCT / HSK Level	
入门第1册 Starter 1	YCT 1	HSK 1
入门第2册 Starter 2	YCT 2	
初级第3册 Beginner 3	YCT 3	HSK 2
初级第4册 Beginner 4		
初级第5册 Beginner 5	YCT 4	HSK 3
初级第6册 Beginner 6		

YCT: 中小学生汉语考试 Youth Chinese Test　　HSK: 汉语水平考试 Chinese Proficiency Test

　　近年来随着"汉语热"的持续升温，越来越多的外国友人热衷于汉语学习。很多国家从中小学就开始汉语教学，同时也有越来越多的中小学学生希望通过参加中国国家汉办的新中小学汉语考试（简称YCT考试）来考查自己在日常生活和学习中运用汉语的能力。为了配合这一趋势，满足中小学汉语教学对教材的需求，在中国国家汉办的指导下，组织国内外教育专家、资深中文教师根据YCT考试大纲编写了《朗朗中文》系列课程的入门级和初级教材。

　　《朗朗中文》系列课程结合海外缺少中文语境、学习时间不多等因素，学习重点是中文听说训练及日常运用，课程力求做到浅显易懂、由浅入深，注重培养学生学习中文的兴趣。

课程套装：

　　《朗朗中文》入门级和初级含1～6册教材，每册分为A、B两套，每套包括课本、练习册、识字卡、在线课程、互动CD-ROM以及《教师用书》和教师字词卡在线打印等。

课程目标：

　　学生完成《朗朗中文》1～6册的学习后，达到YCT四级水平，初步具备"听说读打写"五方面的综合能力。

1. 识读近700个常用字，能理解并使用常用的词语和句子。
2. 可以用中文就熟悉的日常话题进行直接交流。
3. 在中国旅游时，可应对遇到的大部分交际任务。
4. 能独立阅读少儿故事和日常生活、学习中涉及到的中文读物。
5. 能够用中文简单表达自己的观点和情感。
6. 能够用中文进行简单的书写和电脑打字等。

课程结构：

《朗朗中文》1～6册课程以主题为经，单元为纬，每单元两课，围绕一个主题展开"听说读写"教学。每课包含：

1～2册：对话+课堂活动+儿歌+家庭作业（练习册）

3～4册：对话+课堂阅读+课堂练习+儿歌+家庭作业（练习册）

5～6册：对话+课文+课堂练习+文化分享+课外阅读+家庭作业

对话：以学生熟悉的生活和学习环境构建情景，展开对话，训练学生的听说能力。"对话"部分是每课学习的重点，在培养学生中文口头表达能力的同时，将字、词、句融于"对话"中，学习识字、组词和造句。

阅读：3～4册课本中增加了"课堂阅读"，5～6册的练习册中增加了"课外阅读"。阅读内容围绕着朗朗的系列故事展开，是对话部分的情景描写和书面表达。

课文：5～6册每课增加了一篇精读课文，课文反复再现本课学习的生字词和句式。重点训练学生的阅读能力和中文思考能力，学会朗读、默读、诵读，达到"读通、读懂、读好"三个层次的要求。

儿歌：1～4册每课配有一首儿歌，通过采用本课相关的字、词、句改编歌词，让学生唱出课文来，达到增添学生乐趣，活跃课堂气氛的效果。

课堂活动：围绕与课本语言点有关的内容，从听说读写及句式等方面，设计各种课堂游戏或练习，在老师和学生的共同参与下完成。

文化分享：5～6册每单元配有一篇"文化分享"，重点介绍与中国相关的文化常识，让学生初步接触和了解中华文化。

练习册：课本有配套的练习册，供学生课后使用。练习册每课有三页的练习，按每周三天作业量设计，学生可每天完成两页。同时每课还编排了"小测试"，老师可用于课堂测验。

课程特点：

《朗朗中文》1～6册强调中文学习的有效性和实用性，注重语言的交际功能和阅读功能。

1. 注重听说训练，以交际性内容为主导，以听说领先、读写跟上为顺序，强调基础以建立一定的语言习惯。进一步培养实际生活的交际能力、听说读写的语篇能力和全面的跨文化交际能力。

2. 注重字、词、句的有机结合和交叉教学，以字生词、以词组句、以句成篇。同时强调文字的高频复现和句式的反复实践，强化学生的中文记忆和理解能力。

3. 注重"阶梯上升"与"螺旋转进"两种演绎方式，有步骤、分阶段地设计学习重点，从听说、识字到阅读等方面由浅入深，层层递进，使学生的中文学习方式如拾步上梯，学习效果如水到渠成。

4. 教材与YCT考试相匹配，明确学生的学习目标和教师的教学目标，以考促学、以考促教，用一个标准来衡量学生的学习效果和教师的教学效果。同时也为学生提供了一个全新的以学习为主、以考试为辅的中文学习系统。

教学建议：

《朗朗中文》是海外几十年来中文教育的全新突破，因此建议教师学习课程标准，阅读全套教材，钻研整册课文，明确总体教学目标。

1. 关注学生学习中文的兴趣，培养良好的学习习惯。依据教学目标、教材和相关教学资源，合理安排课堂教学内容。

2. 口语交际要通过游戏、表演、体验等课堂活动让学生获得角色认同，明确自己的交际任务。口语交际的教学形式要灵活多样，生动活泼。激发学生听说的兴趣，让学生敢于表达。

3. 识字教学应做到"字不离词，词不离句"，让学生在语境中理解字词的含义。以字义为核心，做到音、形、义相结合。同时要引导学生体会识字方法，多次复现，经常运用，帮助学生掌握生字。

4. 阅读教学应遵循从整体到部分，再回到整体。先初读，理解课文主要内容和思路；再细读，品味语言特色；最后练习、运用。教师要指导学生朗读、默读、诵读，达到读通、读懂、读好。

5. 第4册安排了拼音学习。拼音教学要注重实用性和趣味性，将拼音教学与识字、阅读教学以及拼音打字游戏相结合，同时采用课堂游戏、念儿歌、编口诀等教学形式，提高学生学习拼音的兴趣。

6. 在教学方法上，教师可以根据每课不同的教学内容采用听说法、视听法、认知法等语言教学模式。同时，按照《朗朗中文》课程编辑特点，在课堂上实现知识交叉教学、三步互动教学和反应型记忆教学等三种方法贯穿整个教学过程。

《朗朗中文》课程采用最新中文教学理念和教学方法，运用纸质教材与互联网互动在线课程相结合的教学模式，构建了一个立体的中文教学系统。建议有条件的学校和学生，尽可能充分利用在线课程安排教学和互动学习，通过视听与互动，实现创设中文环境的直观效果。

在《朗朗中文》课程编写过程中，得到了来自美国、加拿大、德国等许多海外中文教师及学生家长的帮助和支持，并提出了大量的建议和意见，在此表示衷心的感谢！

朗朗中文课程编写组

2010年3月

补充说明
Additional Notes

汉语拼音
About Pinyin

Pinyin is printed above the main text, and also in the vocabulary for books One to Six. This will help students engage more with Chinese at the beginning. We also include the non-Pinyin version of the main text for the teacher to use. Pinyin is taught in Book Four.

本教材从第一册起就标注了拼音，其目的是让学生接触拼音，无意识接受并"借助"拼音发音。同时，"你来读一读"中有不加拼音的课文，供老师和学生灵活运用。
拼音课程安排在第四册学习。先接触然后再系统学习拼音，自然水到渠成。中级阶段起课文不再标注拼音。

英文注释
English

English translation is provided for the main text, the vocabulary, and the titles of activities and homework. The online lessons may provide the translations to the other languages used as well.

每课的课文和相关栏目配有英文注释，帮助英语国家的学生理解课文大意，降低对中文理解的难度。

课堂游戏
Classroom Activities

Please refer to the Teacher's Guide for the detailed explanations of Classroom Activities in this book. These activities are developed around the main themes of each unit, and require the teacher's full participation.

《朗朗中文》第一、二册每课后都设计了课堂游戏。游戏内容和游戏形式等在《教师用书》中均有详细说明，请老师参考使用配套的《教师用书》。
课堂练习围绕与本课语言点相关的内容，从听、说、读、写、句式等方面设计，需在课堂上由老师参与完成。

听力练习
Listening Practice

The Listening Practice exercises require the use of audio stored in the online lessons or the CDs. Or the instructor can read aloud the questions found in the Teacher's Guide.

请结合朗朗中文在线课程（www.yes-chinese.com）或课程配套CD-ROM使用。如果学校硬件条件不成熟，不能演示多媒体课程，需由老师亲自朗读听力题目。相关题目和答案全部附在《教师用书》中。

在线课程
Online Courses

Yes! Chinese Online Lessons are an important aspect of the complete curriculum. It's a content rich virtual Chinese language learning environment with many intuitive resources. The online resources are continuously updated.

朗朗中文在线课程设计了更多趣味性、互动性练习，学生可在家长的陪同下一起学习，以增强学生中文学习的兴趣，巩固所学知识。同时在线课程中提供了丰富的中文资源，包括多种中文学习特色栏目。

练习册
Workbook

Each textbook is accompanied by two workbooks, one contains excises for even lessons (the Red Book) while another for odd lessons (the Blue Book). Each lesson comes with 6 pages of excises designed to be completed in three days, and a quiz for classroom assessment. The answer keys for both excises and quiz are provided in online courses.

课本有配套的练习册（单课和双课两本/册），供学生课后使用。每课按每周三天作业量设计，每天两页。同时每课还编排了"小测试"，老师可用于课堂测验。

Curriculum Set 课程套装

Printed Materials 教材

课本
Textbook

练习册
Workbook

识字卡
Flashcards

教师用书
Teachers' Book

Interactive Courses 互动课程

在线课程
Animated Online Courses

课程CD-ROM
Interactive CD-ROM

朗朗中文的最大特色是教材与在线课程结合使用，增加互动，激发兴趣，从而达到更好的中文学习效果。

The unique combination of printed materials and interactive online courses makes Langlang Chinese an intuitive, easy-to-use program that can help students better achieve their learning goals.

CONTENTS 目录

单元四　认识天气
UNIT FOUR　Knowing the Weather

单元目标
STUDY GOAL

听

Listening

理解他人对天气的提问和描述,听懂简单的要求表达。
Understanding inquiries about the weather and understanding simple requests.

说

Speaking

会描述天气,表达自己的要求。
Expressing weather conditions and making requests.

读

Reading & Writing

怎么样	动物园	天气	动物	一起	写
熊猫	老虎	外面	下雨	太阳	
没有	热	冷			

句

Sentence

1. ……怎么样?
2. ……,你呢?
3. 外面在……吗?
4. ……没有……
5. 今天很热。

1

今天天气怎么样?
How Is the Weather Today?

1

jīn tiān de tiān qì zěn me yàng
今天的天气怎么样?

2

jīn tiān tiān qì zhēn hǎo
今天天气真好!

Rabbit Guaiguai: How is the weather today?   **Piggy Beibei:** It is fine today!

3

wǒ yào qù dòng wù yuán kàn xióng māo　nǐ ne
我要去动物园看熊猫，你呢？

4

wǒ yě yào qù dòng wù yuán
我也要去动物园。
wǒ men yī qǐ qù kàn xióng māo
我们一起去看熊猫。

动物表演

爬行馆　熊猫馆

水族馆

Piggy Beibei: I am going to the zoo, and you?
Rabbit Guaiguai: I will go with you. Let's go to see the pandas.

3

乖乖兔：今天的天气怎么样？

贝贝猪：今天天气真好！

贝贝猪：我要去动物园看熊猫，你呢？

乖乖兔：我也要去动物园。
　　　　我们一起去看熊猫。

zěn	yàng	dòng	wù	yuán	xióng
怎	样	动	物	园	熊

词汇
New Words

tiān qì	zěn me yàng	dòng wù	dòng wù yuán
天气	怎么样	动物	动物园
weather	how	animals	zoo

xióng māo	yì qǐ
熊猫	一起
panda	together

句式
Sentences

今天的天气怎么样?

我要去动物园看熊猫,你呢?

第1题 识字游戏

Train Ride

开火车

火车火车哪里开?
火车火车这里开。

第2题 课堂游戏

Card Game

叠词成句

老师读句子，学生找出字卡
按句子顺序贴在黑板上。

园　我　好　熊　去　今　动

6

lǎo hǔ
老 虎
tiger

1. 两人一组，仿照下列情景进行对话表演。

A：这儿的天气怎么样？
B：这儿的天气真好！
A：我要去动物园，你呢？
B：我也要去。我要看老虎。

2. 选词填空，说一说句子的意思。

_____ 天气怎么样？（今天 / 明天 / ……）

_____ 的天气怎么样？（这儿 / 那儿 / 北京 / ……）

第4题

听声音，选词语。
Listening to the audio, write down the letter next to the word your hear in the blank space.

Ⓐ 小猫　Ⓑ 小狗　Ⓒ 老虎　Ⓓ 小鱼　Ⓔ 小鸟　Ⓕ 熊猫

EXAMPLE 例 EXAMPLE　◀)) 小鸟　**E**　① ____　② ____　③ ____　④ ____　⑤ ____

第5~7题

听声音，选句子。
Listening to the audio, write down the letter next to the sentence you hear in the blank space.

EXAMPLE 例 EXAMPLE　◀)) 今天天气真好。
Ⓐ 今天天气真好。　Ⓑ 今天天气不好。　（ **A** ）

5. Ⓐ 他们去看熊猫。　Ⓑ 他们去看老虎。　（　）

6. Ⓐ 今天天气怎么样？　Ⓑ 明天天气怎么样？　（　）

7. Ⓐ 我和朗朗一起去商店。　Ⓑ 我和小米一起去学校。（　）

7

选字组词。
Select words from the word box, and then draw lines to link them with the fans below to create appropriate new phrases. Each word can only be used once.

Ⓐ 书　　Ⓑ 红　　Ⓒ 面　　Ⓓ 里　　Ⓔ 上

Ⓕ 黄　　Ⓖ 条　　Ⓗ 子　　Ⓘ 绿

看图判断对错。对的请打"✓"，错的请打"✗"。
True or False.

 今天天气真好！ Ⓧ

9. 他们一起去动物园。 ✓

10. 他们在看老虎。 ✗

11. 朗朗在玩电脑。 ✓

12. 书包是黄色的。

8

写出正确的序号组成句子。
Write down the letter of each phrase in the correct order as the sentences.

例 ① 要　② 也　③ 去　④ 我　⑤ 学校

④ ② ① ③ ⑤。

---

13. ① 天气　② 怎么样　③ 今天

_____?

14. ① 真好　② 这儿　③ 天气　④ 的

_____!

15. ① 我和朗朗　② 动物园　③ 一起　④ 去

_____。

唱响中文
SING ALONG
www.yes-chinese.com

两只老虎

两只老虎，两只老虎，
跑得快！跑得快！
一只没有耳朵，一只没有尾巴。
真奇怪！真奇怪！

须使用课程CD-ROM或在线课程（www.yes-chinese.com），跟着音乐演唱。
This lyric should be sung along with the music found in the course CD-ROM or in the online lessons.

9

外面在下雨吗？
Is It Raining Outside?

1

wài miàn zài xià yǔ ma
外面在下雨吗？

2

wài miàn méi yǒu xià yǔ
外面没有下雨。

3

wài miàn yǒu tài yáng ma
外面有太阳吗？

4

yǒu   jīn tiān hěn rè
有。今天很热。

Langlang: Is it raining outside?
Xiaomi: It isn't raining.

Langlang: Is it sunny outside?
Xiaomi: Yes, it is very hot today.

Langlang: I am going swimming, and you?   **Xiaomi:** I am going shopping.

11

你来读一读
YOUR TURN

朗朗：外面在下雨吗？

小米：外面没有下雨。

朗朗：外面有太阳吗？

小米：有。今天很热。

朗朗：我要去游泳，你呢？

小米：我要去商店。

生字
New Characters

wài	xià	yǔ	tài	yáng	rè
外	下	雨	太	阳	热

词汇
New Words

wài miàn	xià yǔ	tài yáng	méi yǒu
外面	下雨	太阳	没有
outside	raining	sun	not

句式
Sentences

外面在下雨吗？

外面没有下雨。

今天很热。

第 1 题　识字游戏　找朋友。
Find Friends

第 2 题　拓展训练

A：外面在下雨吗？

B：外面在下雨。今天很冷。

A：我在家看电视，你呢？

B：我要画画儿。

lěng

冷
cold

第 3 题　课堂游戏　看图说话。
Picture Talking

14

第 4 题　听声音，选字词。
Listening to the audio, write down the letter next to the word you hear in the blank space.

Ⓐ 太阳　　Ⓑ 下雨　　Ⓒ 外面　　Ⓓ 里面　　Ⓔ 没有

Ⓕ 冷　　Ⓖ 热

 🔊 没有 ___E___

① _____　　② _____　　③ _____　　④ _____　　⑤ _____　　⑥ _____

第 5~9 题　听声音，判断对错。对的请打"✓"，错的请打"✗"。
Listening to the audio, and mark "√" in the blank space if the statement matches the picture, or "✕" if it does not.

 🔊 天气真好！ ✔

5. ◯

6. ◯

7. ◯

8. ◯

9. ◯

15

圈反义词。
Circle the antonyms.

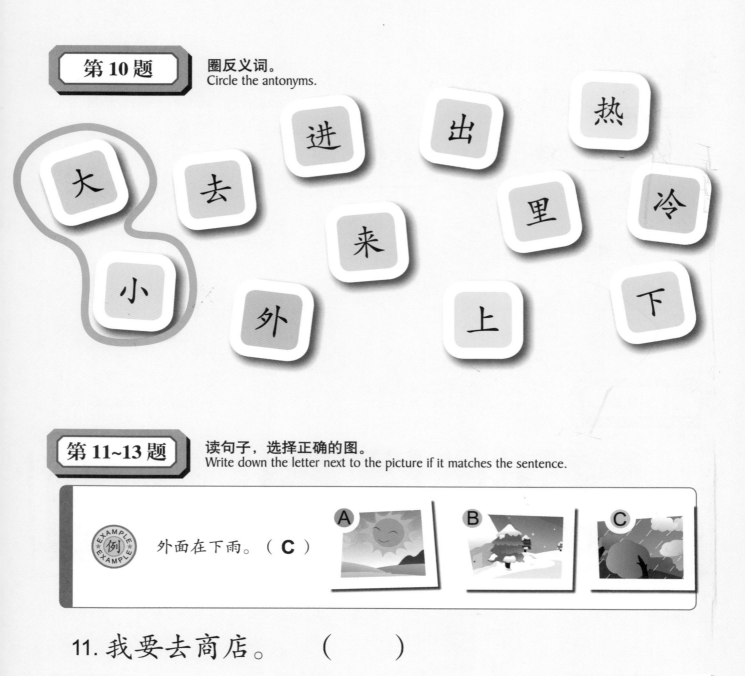

大　小

去

进

出

热

来

里

冷

外

上

下

第 11~13 题

读句子，选择正确的图。
Write down the letter next to the picture if it matches the sentence.

例 EXAMPLE 　外面在下雨。（ **C** ）

Ⓐ　Ⓑ　Ⓒ

11. 我要去商店。　（　　）

12. 我要去游泳。（　　）

 A

 B

 C

13. 今天很热。　（　　）

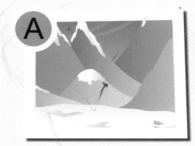 A

 B

 C

第 14~16 题　写出正确的序号组成句子。
Write down the letter of each phrase in the correct order as the sentences.

EXAMPLE 例 EXAMPLE　❶ 下雨　❷ 外面　❸ 没有
② ③ ① 。

14. ❶ 热　　❷ 今天　　❸ 很

_____。

15. ❶ 吗　　❷ 外面　　❸ 在　　❹ 下雨

_____?

16. ❶ 太阳　　❷ 有　　❸ 吗　　❹ 外面

_____?

读书郎

小嘛小儿郎，背着那书包上学堂，
不怕太阳晒，不怕那风雨狂。
不怕那天气热和冷呀，
我要读书哟，一天天成长。

单元五　买东西
UNIT FIVE　Shopping

第九课　这个多少钱？
Lesson 9　How Much Is This?

第十课　她买了一个杯子
Lesson 10　She Bought a Cup

听

Listening

听懂他人表达价钱，听懂他人买的什么东西和用处。
Understanding the expressions of price from others and understanding the exact shoppping item and the use.

说

Speaking

会用中文问价钱、买东西。
Asking about prices and shopping.

读

Reading & Writing

钱	块	两
铅笔	多少	东西
昨天	杯子	喝茶
弟弟	妹妹	

了
衣服
送给

句

Sentence

1. ……多少钱？
2. ……和……一起……
3. ……了……

19

第九课
Lesson 9

这个多少钱?
How Much Is This?

1

wǒ yào qù mǎi shū bāo hé qiān bǐ
我要去买书包和铅笔。

2

wǒ hé nǐ yì qǐ qù shāng diàn
我和你一起去商店。

3

zhè ge shū bāo duō shao qián
这个书包多少钱?

4

shí wǔ kuài
十五块。

Rabbit Guaiguai: I am going to buy a bag and a pencil.
Piggy Beibei: I will go shopping with you.

Rabbit Guaiguai: How much is this bag?
Salesclerk: Fifteen Yuan.

20

5

qiān bǐ ne
铅笔呢？

6

liǎng kuài
两块。

7

shū bāo hé qiān bǐ wǒ dōu mǎi
书包和铅笔我都买。

8

hǎo de
好的。

Rabbit Guaiguai: How much is this pencil?
Salesclerk: Two Yuan.

Rabbit Guaiguai: I will take both the bag and the pencil.
Salesclerk: Okay.

乖乖兔：我要去买书包和铅笔。

贝贝猪：我和你一起去商店。

乖乖兔：这个书包多少钱？

售货员：十五块。

乖乖兔：铅笔呢？

售货员：两块。

乖乖兔：书包和铅笔我都买。

售货员：好的。

qiān	bǐ	shǎo	qián	kuài	liǎng
铅	笔	少	钱	块	两

词汇
New Words

qiān bǐ	duō shao
铅笔	多少
pencil	how much

句式
Sentences

这个书包多少钱？

我和你一起去商店。

23

课堂活动
Classroom Activities
Refer to your Teacher's Guide for activity details.

第1题 识字游戏

Rock Shooting

登火箭

用彩纸做三枚火箭竖着贴在黑板上。

第2题 课堂游戏

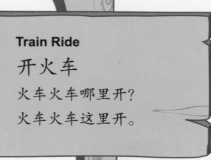

Train Ride

开火车

火车火车哪里开?
火车火车这里开。

两人一组，一人扮演售货员，一人扮演顾客，用身边的物品表演购物。
Two as a group, one acts as the cashier while the other as the customer, perform shopping situation by using the objects around you.

A: 你要买什么东西？

B: 我要买衣服。

A: 红色的衣服怎么样？

B: 真漂亮！多少钱？

A: 三十块。

dōng xi
东 西
stuff

yī fu
衣 服
clothes

第4题　听声音，选词语。
Listening to the audio, write down the letter next to the word you hear in the blank space.

Ⓐ 东西　Ⓑ 衣服　Ⓒ 铅笔　Ⓓ 书包　Ⓔ 多少

🔊 衣服 __B__　① _____　② _____　③ _____　④ _____

第5~8题　听声音，选择正确的答案。
Listening to the audio, write down the letter of the answer key in the blank space.

🔊 书包十五块。
Ⓐ 二十块　Ⓑ 十五块　Ⓒ 八块　（ **B** ）

5. Ⓐ 一块　Ⓑ 两块　Ⓒ 四块　（　）

6. Ⓐ 十块　Ⓑ 二十块　Ⓒ 四十块　（　）

7. Ⓐ 两块　Ⓑ 三块　Ⓒ 四块　（　）

8. Ⓐ 三块　Ⓑ 四块　Ⓒ 五块　（　）

25

把类型相同的词连起来。
Link the words with the same type.

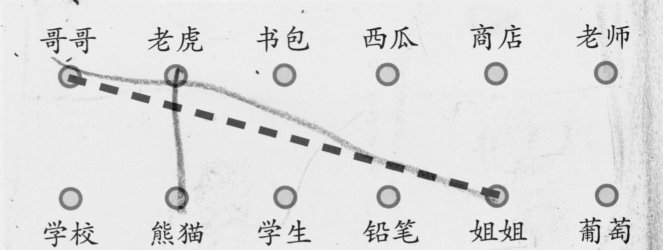

哥哥　　老虎　　书包　　西瓜　　商店　　老师

学校　　熊猫　　学生　　铅笔　　姐姐　　葡萄

看图完成对话。
Count the money and write the exact amount in Chinese.

例 EXAMPLE

问：✎ + ◺ 多少钱？　　答：__三__ 块。

10. 问：✎ + ◺ + ▬ 多少钱？

答：____ 块。

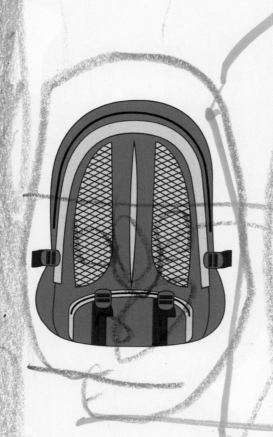
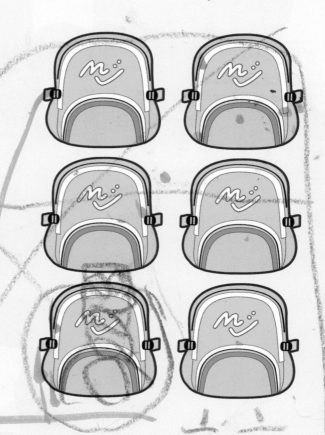

11. 问： 黄书包有几个？　答：＿＿＿＿个。 六 6

12. 问： 红书包有几个？　答：＿＿＿＿个。 一

13. 问： 黄书包和红书包，哪个多？哪个少？

答： 黄书包＿＿＿＿，红书包＿＿＿＿。 多少

14. 问： 黄书包＋红书包，有多少个？

答： 黄书包＋红书包有＿七＿个。 七

读句子或对话，选择正确的字词。
Write down the letter of the word that best completes the sentence.

 姐姐很爱 __B__ 画儿。
Ⓐ 说　　Ⓑ 画　　Ⓒ 打

15. 他的哥哥是一个 ___C___ 。

Ⓐ 同学　　　　Ⓑ 朋友　　　　Ⓒ 学生

16. 他们在 ___A___ 电话。

Ⓐ 打　　　　Ⓑ 玩　　　　Ⓒ 看

17. ___C___ 里有很多漂亮的衣服。

Ⓐ 动物园　　Ⓑ 学校　　　Ⓒ 商店

18. 男：我可以坐在这儿吗？
　　女：可以。
　　男：_____ 。

Ⓐ 谢谢　　　Ⓑ 对不起　　Ⓒ 没关系

19. 这件衣服 ___C___ 钱？

Ⓐ 很大　　　Ⓑ 很多　　　Ⓒ 多少

大小多少

一个大，一个小，

一只老虎一只猫，

一只老虎一只猫。

一个多，一个少，

很多铅笔一个书包。

须使用课程CD-ROM或在线课程（www.yes-chinese.com），跟着音乐演唱。
This lyric should be sung along with the music found in the course CD-ROM or in the online lessons.

29

她买了一个杯子
She Bought a Cup

1

guāi guai tù zuó tiān qù le nǎ er
乖乖兔昨天去了哪儿？

2

tā zuó tiān qù le shāng diàn　　tā mǎi le yí gè bēi zi
她昨天去了商店。她买了一个杯子。

Langlang: Where did Rabbit Guaiguai go yesterday?
Xiaomi: She went shopping yesterday, and bought a cup.

tā mǎi bēi zi zuò shén me
她买杯子做什么？

sòng gěi tā bà ba　　tā bà ba
送给她爸爸。她爸爸

xǐ huan hē chá
喜欢喝茶。

Langlang: For what?
Xiaomi: She gave it to her father. Her father likes drinking tea.

31

你来读一读
YOUR TURN

朗朗：乖乖兔昨天去了哪儿？

小米：她昨天去了商店。
　　　她买了一个杯子。

朗朗：她买杯子做什么？

小米：送给她爸爸。
　　　她爸爸喜欢喝茶。

zuó	le	bēi	sòng	gěi	chá
昨	了	杯	送	给	茶

词汇
New Words

zuó tiān	bēi zi	sòng gěi	hē chá
昨天	杯子	送给	喝茶
yesterday	cup	send to	drink tea

句式
Sentences

她昨天去了哪儿？

33

课堂活动
Classroom Activities
Refer to your Teacher's Guide for activity details.

第 1 题 识字游戏

昨天

喝茶

杯子

送给

多少

第 2 题 课堂游戏

34

两人一组，仿照下列情景进行对话练习。
Following the examples below, find a partner and create a dialogue.

A：你昨天去了哪里？

B：昨天很冷，我在家看电视。

A：我没有看电视。我去了商店。

B：你买了什么？

A：我买了铅笔送给弟弟。
　　我买了书包送给妹妹。

dì	di		mèi	mei
弟	弟		妹	妹

younger brother　　younger sister

果汁

面包

米饭

A：你昨天吃了 面条 吗？

B：我昨天没吃 面条，
　　我吃了 米饭。

A：你今天喝了 牛奶 吗？

B：我今天没喝 牛奶，
　　我喝了 果汁。

A：你明天要吃什么？

B：明天？我想吃 面包。

第 4 题

听声音，选词语。
Listening to the audio, write down the letter next to the word you hear in the blank space.

Ⓐ 喝茶　　Ⓑ 杯子　　Ⓒ 妹妹　　Ⓓ 商店　　Ⓔ 学校　　Ⓕ 送给

 🔊 妹妹 __C__

① _____　　② _____　　③ _____　　④ _____　　⑤ _____

第 5~8 题

听声音，选句子。
Listening to the audio, write down the letter next to the sentence you hear in the bracket.

🔊 他今天去了学校。

Ⓐ 他昨天去了学校。　　Ⓑ 他今天去了学校。（　**B**　）

5. Ⓐ 弟弟喜欢玩电脑。　　Ⓑ 妹妹喜欢看电视。　　（　　　）

6. Ⓐ 她买杯子做什么？　　Ⓑ 她买书包做什么？　　（　　　）

7. Ⓐ 他买了一个杯子。　　Ⓑ 她买了两个杯子。　　（　　　）

8. Ⓐ 杯子送给弟弟。　　Ⓑ 书包送给妹妹。　　（　　　）

第 9 题

选出可以和"喝"、"吃"组成短语的字词。
Circle the words that can make compound words with "喝" and "吃".

Ⓐ 米饭　　Ⓑ 面包　　Ⓒ 茶　　Ⓓ 面条　　Ⓔ 水

Ⓕ 苹果　　Ⓖ 牛奶

喝：__C__　　　　　　　吃：__A__

看图判断对错。对的请打"✓"，错的请打"✗"。
True or False.

喝茶 ✓

10. 弟弟 ◯

11. 妹妹 ✗

12. 杯子 ✗

13. 喝水 ✗

写出正确的序号组成句子。
Write down the letter of each word in the correct order as the sentences.

例 EXAMPLE ❶ 我   ❷ 喝   ❸ 茶   ❹ 喜欢
① ④ ② ③ 。

14. ❶ 杯子   ❷ 她   ❸ 买了   ❹ 两个
_____ 。

15. ❶ 没去   ❷ 昨天   ❸ 小米   ❹ 学校
_____ 。

16. ❶ 书包   ❷ 朗朗   ❸ 做什么   ❹ 买
_____ ?

二十五块

我在商店里，买了米和面，
把它送给爸爸妈妈手里边。
妈妈把头点，问我多少钱？
我高兴地对她说："二十五块。"

单元六　看医生
UNIT SIX　See a Doctor

第十一课　他怎么了？
Lesson 11　What Is the Matter With Him?

第十二课　你觉得怎么样？
Lesson 12　How Do You Feel?

单元目标
STUDY GOAL

听 Listening

理解他人对状态的提问和表达，听懂时间的表达。
Understanding expressions of concern from others and understanding expressions of time.

说 Speaking

会问他人的状态，表达自己的状态，能使用更多的时间表达。
Asking how others are doing, expressing how you are doing; as well as more ways of expressing time.

读 Reading & Writing

疼	半	早上	医院
医生	怎么	房间	睡觉
觉得	晚上	分钟	北京

句 Sentence

1. ……怎么了？
2. 不要……
3. ……觉得……
4. ……要不要……？

第十一课 Lesson 11

他怎么了?
What Is the Matter With Him?

1
jīn tiān zǎo shang nǐ qù le nǎ er
今天早上你去了哪儿?

2
wǒ hé bèi bei zhū qù le yī yuàn
我和贝贝猪去了医院。

3
nǐ men zěn me le
你们怎么了?

4
bèi bei zhū qù kàn yī shēng
贝贝猪去看医生。

Xiaomi: Where did you go in the morning?
Langlang: I went to the hospital with Beibei.

Xiaomi: What is wrong with you?
Langlang: Beibei went to see the doctor.

Xiaomi: How is he now?   **Langlang:** Shush! He is sleeping in the room.

小米：今天早上你去了哪儿？

朗朗：我和贝贝猪去了医院。

小米：你们怎么了？

朗朗：贝贝猪去看医生。

小米：他现在怎么样？

朗朗：不要说话！他在房间睡觉。

生字
New Characters

zǎo	yī	yuàn	fáng	jiān
早	医	院	房	间

shuì	jiào
睡	觉

词汇
New Words

zǎo shang	yī yuàn	zěn me	yī shēng
早上	医院	怎么	医生
early morning	hospital	how	doctor

fáng jiān	shuì jiào
房间	睡觉
house	sleep

句式
Sentences

你们怎么了?

不要说话!

43

第 1 题 识字游戏

第 2 题 课堂游戏

Find Friends

找朋友

我的朋友在哪里？
你的朋友在这里。

44

想一想，试着理解下列每组句子的意思有什么不同。
Figure out the meaning of the sentences in each group.

1 你怎么了？
你怎么样？

5 外面怎么了？
外面天气怎么样？

2 请进来。
不要进来。

6 请喝茶。
不要喝茶。

3 她去了商店。
她要去商店。

7 我买了一个书包。
我在买书包。

4 她会唱歌。
她不会唱歌。

8 他不会说汉语。
他会不会说汉语？

第4题

听声音，选词语。
Listening to the audio, write down the letter next to the word you hear in the blank space.

Ⓐ 早上　Ⓑ 医院　Ⓒ 医生　Ⓓ 睡觉　Ⓔ 怎么　Ⓕ 房间

　🔊 早上　**A**

① _____　② _____　③ _____　④ _____　⑤ _____

第5~9题

听声音，判断对错。对的请打"✓"，错的请打"✗"。
Listening to the audio, and mark "√" in the blank space if the statement matches the picture, or an "✕" if it doesn't.

🔊 看医生 ✓

5. ✗

6. ○

7. ○

8. ✗

9. ✗

看图判断对错。对的请打"✓"，错的请打"✗"。
Read the sentence,mark a "√" in the circle if the picture matches, or an "×" if it doesn't.

 他在看医生。

10. 她买杯子。

11. 他在喝水。

12. 不要说话！

13. 她在睡觉。

看图连线。
Connect the phrases to the corresponding pictures.

医生　　熊猫　　老师　　老虎　　睡觉　　学生

○　　　○　　　●　　　○　　　○　　　○

○　　　○　　　○　　　○

读句子，选择正确的回答。
Write down the letter next to the phrase that best answers each question.

Ⓐ 看老虎。　　Ⓑ 睡觉。　　Ⓒ 学中文。　　Ⓓ 看医生。

 他去医院做什么？（ **D** ）

15. 他去学校做什么？　　（　　）

16. 他去动物园做什么？　　（　　）

17. 他去房间做什么？　　（　　）

怎么了？

贝贝猪，怎么了？
今天没有来学校。
我问朗朗知不知道，
朗朗说："贝贝猪现在在睡觉。"

你觉得怎么样?
How Do You Feel?

1

bèi bei zhū nǐ jué de
贝贝猪，你觉得
zěn me yàng
怎么样？

2

tóu hěn téng
头很疼。

3

nǐ yào bu yào qù kàn yī shēng
你要不要去看医生？

4

wǒ yào qù kàn yī shēng
我要去看医生。

Langlang: How are you feeling now, Beibei?
Piggy Beibei: I have a headache.

Langlang: Would you like to see the doctor?
Piggy Beibei: Yes. I would.

5 xiàn zài jǐ diǎn le
现在几点了？

6 xiàn zài shì wǎn shang qī diǎn èr shí fēn
现在是晚上七点二十分。

7 qī diǎn bàn wǒ hé nǐ yì qǐ qù yī yuàn
七点半我和你一起去医院。

8 hǎo xiè xie
好。谢谢！

Langlang: What time is it now?
Piggy Beibei: It is twenty past seven.

Langlang: Let's go to the hospital at half past seven.
Piggy Beibei: Okay, Thank you!

朗朗：贝贝猪，你觉得怎么样？

贝贝猪：头很疼。

朗朗：你要不要去看医生？

贝贝猪：我要去看医生。

朗朗：现在几点了？

贝贝猪：现在是晚上七点二十分。

朗朗：七点半我和你一起去医院。

贝贝猪：好。谢谢！

jué	dé	téng	wǎn	fēn	bàn
觉	得	疼	晚	分	半

词汇
New Words

jué de	wǎn shang
觉得	晚上
feel	night

句式
Sentences

你觉得怎么样?

你要不要去看医生?

53

课堂活动
Classroom Activities
Refer to your Teacher's Guide for activity details.

第 1 题 识字游戏

Train Ride

开火车
火车火车哪里开?
火车火车这里开。

第 2 题 课堂游戏

Group Singing

丢手绢
学生围成一圈蹲在地上，大家拍手唱歌。

两人一组，仿照下列情景进行对话练习。
Following the examples below, find a partner and create a dialogue.

医生：你怎么了？

病人：我头疼。

医生：我看看。嗯……没关系，
回家睡二十分钟就好了。

病人：谢谢！

fēn　zhōng
分　钟
minutes

běi　jīng
北　京
Beijing

A：你去了哪里？
B：我去了北京。
A：你觉得北京怎么样？
B：我觉得北京很漂亮。

第4～6题

看图写时间或按照时间画图。
Write and Draw.

EXAMPLE 例

七 点 二十 分

4. ＿＿＿＿ 点 ＿＿＿＿

（＿＿ 点 ＿＿ 分）

5. 十二点十分

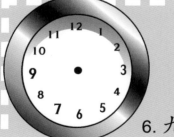

6. 九点五十分

**第 7~10 题**　听声音，选词语。
Listening to the audio, write down the letter next to the word you hear in the bracket.

> 例 ◀) 觉得
> Ⓐ 睡觉　　Ⓑ 觉得　　Ⓒ 头疼（　**B**　）

7. Ⓐ 早上　　　　Ⓑ 上边　　　　Ⓒ 晚上　　（　　　）

8. Ⓐ 昨天　　　　Ⓑ 今天　　　　Ⓒ 明天　　（　　　）

9. Ⓐ 学生　　　　Ⓑ 医生　　　　Ⓒ 医院　　（　　　）

10. Ⓐ 中国　　　　Ⓑ 美国　　　　Ⓒ 北京　　（　　　）

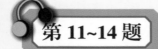**第 11~14 题**　听声音，选句子。
Listening to the audio, write down the letter next to the sentence you hear in the bracket.

> ◀) 你觉得北京怎么样？
> Ⓐ 你觉得北京怎么样？　　Ⓑ 你觉得中国怎么样？（　**A**　）

11. Ⓐ 要不要去学校？　　Ⓑ 要不要去医院？　（　　　）

12. Ⓐ 早上我要上学。　　Ⓑ 晚上我要睡觉。　（　　　）

13. Ⓐ 现在是七点二十分。
　　Ⓑ 现在是七点四十分。　　　　　　　　（　　　）

14. Ⓐ 他妈妈是老师。　　Ⓑ 他爸爸是医生。　（　　　）

第 15~19 题　读对话，选择对应的图。
Write down the letter next to the picture that best describes the conversation.

A

B

C

D

E

F

　问：你觉得北京怎么样？　　答：很漂亮。（ **D** ）

15. 问：她现在怎么样？　答：不要说话！她在睡觉。（　　）

16. 问：早上你去了哪儿？　　答：我去了医院。（　　）

17. 问：你爸爸喜欢喝茶吗？　答：是的。（　　）

18. 问：她怎么了？　　　　　答：她头很疼。（　　）

19. 问：你们昨天去了哪儿？

答：我们去了动物园。（　　）

睡觉睡到大天亮

贝贝猪的头很疼呀，
要不要去看医生呀？
今天晚上七点半啊，
我们送他去医院呀。

到了医院看医生哪，
医生说啊没关系呀。
现在觉得怎么样啊？
睡觉睡到大天亮啊。

单元七　假期生活
UNIT SEVEN　Holidays

单元目标
STUDY GOAL

第十三课　我学习画画儿两年了
Lesson 13　I Have Learned Painting for Two Years

第十四课　中国人很多
Lesson 14　There Are So Many People in China

听

Listening

听懂他人的时间、要求、意愿、行为表达，理解他人的比较。
Understanding the expressions of time, demands, desires, and behaviors, as well as expressing comparisons.

说

Speaking

能使用更多的时间、要求、意愿、行为表达，会进行比较。
Using more expressions related to time, demands, desires, and behaviors, as well as making comparisons.

读

Reading & Writing

起床　下午
电影　椅子
上海　多久

弹钢琴　比
放假　地方

写

句

Sentence

1. ……学习……（多久）了。
2. ……比……

59

我学习画画儿两年了
I Have Learned Painting for Two Years

1

nǐ míng tiān zǎo shang jǐ diǎn qǐ chuáng
你明天早上几点起床？

2

wǒ qī diǎn sì shí wǔ
我七点四十五
qǐ chuáng
起床。

3

zǎo shang nǐ yào zuò shén me ne
早上你要做什么呢？

4

wǒ yào xué huà huà er
我要学画画儿。
wǒ xué xí huà huà er liǎng nián le
我学习画画儿两年了。

Langlang: What time will you get up tomorrow?
Xiaomi: I get up at a quarter to eight.

Langlang: What will you do in the morning?
Xiaomi: I have to draw. I have learned drawing for two years.

Langlang: What will you do in the afternoon?

Xiaomi: I have to play the piano.

Langlang: How about the evening? Will you go to the cinema with me?

Xiaomi: I am sorry, I can't. Beibei will come to my house this evening.

朗朗：你明天早上几点起床？

小米：我七点四十五起床。

朗朗：早上你要做什么呢？

小米：我要学画画儿。我学习画画儿
　　　两年了。

朗朗：下午你要做什么？

小米：我要弹钢琴。

朗朗：晚上呢？可以和我去看电影吗？

小米：对不起，贝贝猪要来我家玩。

chuáng	wǔ	tán	gāng	qín	yǐng
床	午	弹	钢	琴	影

词汇
New Words

qǐ chuáng	xià wǔ	gāng qín	diàn yǐng
起 床	下 午	钢琴	电影
get up	afternoon	piano	movie

句式
Sentences

我学习画画儿两年了。

63

课堂活动
Classroom Activities
Refer to your Teacher's Guide for activity details.

第1题 识字游戏

找尾巴：请同学们给动物找尾巴，并读一读尾巴上的生字。
Find the Tails: Read the words on each animal's tail.

床　影　午　弹　钢　琴

第2题 课堂游戏

抢椅子。

1. 我明天八点半去学校。
2. 我喜欢这个小椅子，真漂亮！
3. 乖乖兔学唱歌十个月了。
4. 小米学游泳两个星期了。
5. 我和妈妈晚上七点五十分去看电影。

yǐ　zi

椅 子

chair

仿照例句，用下列词组进行选词叠句比赛。
Following the example, use the giving key words to create your own sentences, each time expanding the sentences a bit.

椅子/桌子/起床/电影/画画儿/北京/漂亮/我们/弹钢琴

例：椅——椅子——坐椅子——我坐在椅子上弹钢琴。

　　桌——桌子——在桌子上——我们在桌子上画画儿。

64

听声音，判断对错。对的请打"✓"，错的请打"✗"。
Listening to the audio, mark a "√" in the circle if the picture matches, or an "×" if it doesn't.

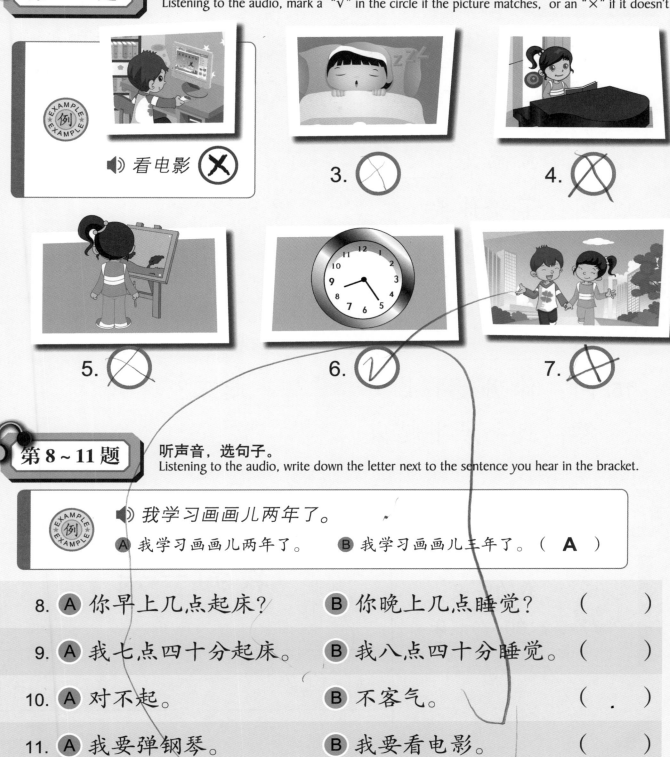

看电影 ✗

3. ⊘

4. ⊘

5. ⊘

6. ✓

7. ⊘

听声音，选句子。
Listening to the audio, write down the letter next to the sentence you hear in the bracket.

例 ◀) 我学习画画儿两年了。

Ⓐ 我学习画画儿两年了。　　Ⓑ 我学习画画儿三年了。（ **A** ）

8. Ⓐ 你早上几点起床？　　Ⓑ 你晚上几点睡觉？（　　）

9. Ⓐ 我七点四十分起床。　　Ⓑ 我八点四十分睡觉。（　　）

10. Ⓐ 对不起。　　Ⓑ 不客气。（　.　）

11. Ⓐ 我要弹钢琴。　　Ⓑ 我要看电影。（　　）

读句子或对话，选择正确的词语。
Find the words on the list that best completes each sentence. Write down the letter in the blank space.

Ⓐ 做什么　　Ⓑ 两年　　Ⓒ 对不起　　Ⓓ 几点　　Ⓔ 看医生

 问：你要不要去__E__?　　答：是的，我要去。

12. 我学画画儿 _____ 了。

13. 问：下午你要 _____?
    答：我要学习弹钢琴。

14. 问：晚上和我去唱歌吗?
    答：_____，我要看电视。

15. 问：你明天早上 _____ 起床?
    答：我七点半起床。

第 16 题　　写一写你的一天。
Writing Practice.

我的一天
7:30　　起床

我的一天

_____

_____

_____

请把与"电影、画画儿、哥哥、床"类型相同的词语分别放进圆圈里。
Classify the Words.

A 桌子　　　　**B** 弹钢琴　　　　**C** 唱歌　　　　**D** 电视

E 妹妹　　　　**F** 电脑　　　　**G** 椅子　　　　**H** 姐姐

I 电话　　　　**J** 游泳　　　　**K** 弟弟

电影　　　　D

画画儿

哥哥

床

我们真高兴

画画儿，弹钢琴，我弹钢琴给你听。

玩电脑，看电影，假期过得真开心。

你要去上海，我要去北京，

我们的心里，真高兴！

须使用课程CD-ROM或在线课程（www.yes-chinese.com），跟着音乐演唱。
This lyric should be sung along with the music found in the course CD-ROM or in the online lessons.

67

中国人很多
There Are So Many People in China

1

fàng jià le nǐ yào qù nǎ er
放假了你要去哪儿？

2

wǒ yào qù zhōng guó
我要去中国。

3

zhōng guó rén hěn duō　　zhōng guó rén
中国人很多。中国人
bǐ měi guó rén duō
比美国人多。

Xiaomi: Where will you go this holiday?
Langlang: I will go to China.

Langlang: China has a large population. The Chinese population is bigger than America's.

Xiaomi: China is a large country. Where will you go?
Langlang: I will go to Beijing and Shanghai.

Xiaomi: How long will you stay?
Langlang: Three weeks.

小米：放假了你要去哪儿？

朗朗：我要去中国。

朗朗：中国人很多。中国人比美国人多。

小米：中国很大，你要去几个地方？

朗朗：我要去两个地方，北京和上海。

小米：你要去多久？

朗朗：三个星期。

生字
New Characters

fàng	jià	bǐ	dì	fāng
放	假	比	地	方

hǎi	jiǔ
海	久

词汇
New Words

fàng jià	dì fang	shàng hǎi	duō jiǔ
放假	地方	上海	多久
holiday	place	Shanghai	how long

句式
Sentences

中国人比美国人多。

第1题 识字游戏

摘苹果。
Apple Picking

第2题 课堂游戏

例句：

1. 他（的个子）比我高。
2. 我的手比他的小。
3. 我的头发比她的长。
4. 他比我大一岁。我比他小一岁。

Find Friends

集体舞"找朋友"
全班学生分为两队，按内外圈绕着小树
一边唱《找朋友》，一边跳舞。
仿照例句说话。

 第3题

听声音，选词语。
Listening to the audio, write down the letter next to the word you hear in the blank space.

A 放假　　B 北京　　C 上海　　D 中国　　E 美国

F 多久　　G 地方

 🔊 多久 ___F___

① _____　② _____　③ _____　④ _____　⑤ _____　⑥ _____

第4~7题

听声音，选图片。对的请打 " √ " 。
Listening to the audio, mark a "√" in the circle if the picture matches.

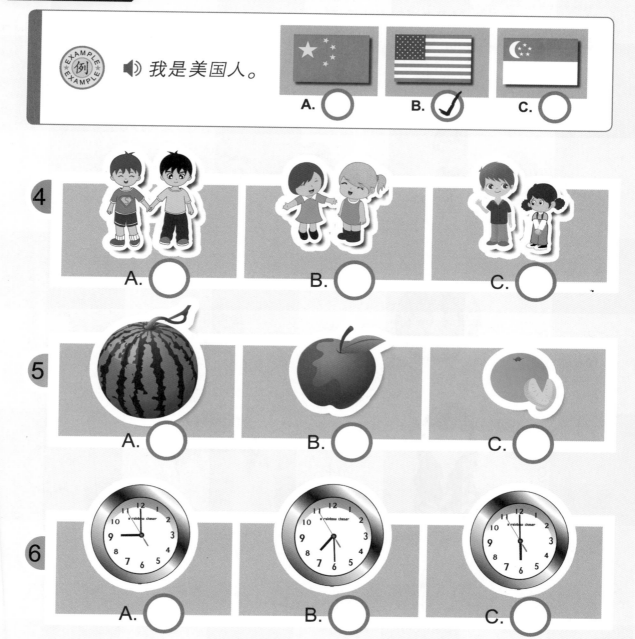

EXAMPLE 例 EXAMPLE 🔊 我是美国人。

A. ○   B. ✓   C. ○

4 A. ○   B. ○   C. ○

5 A. ○   B. ○   C. ○

6 A. ○   B. ○   C. ○

7

A. ○   B. ○   C. ○

看图选择正确的词语。
Find the words on the list that best describes the picture, then write the letter in the circle.

Ⓐ 多　　Ⓑ 高　　Ⓒ 长　　Ⓓ 大　　Ⓔ 小

例　　比　　Ⓑ

8.　　比　　◯

9.　　比　　◯

10.　　比　　◯

11.　　比　　◯

读句子，选择正确的字词。
Write down the letter next to the word that best completes the sentence.

EXAMPLE 例 EXAMPLE

早上，我 __C__ 了一个包子。
Ⓐ 说　Ⓑ 喝　Ⓒ 吃

12. 今天比昨天 ____。
Ⓐ 太阳　　Ⓑ 热　　Ⓒ 下雨

13. 妈妈 ____ 我一个漂亮的书包。
Ⓐ 要　　Ⓑ 买　　Ⓒ 送

14. 买了新衣服，我很 ____。
Ⓐ 好　　Ⓑ 疼　　Ⓒ 高兴

15. 小米在 _____ 钢琴。

Ⓐ 打　　　　　Ⓑ 弹　　　　　Ⓒ 玩

16. 我坐在 _____ 上画画儿。

Ⓐ 这里　　　　Ⓑ 房间　　　　Ⓒ 椅子

17. 放假了你要去什么 _____？

Ⓐ 东西　　　　Ⓑ 地方　　　　Ⓒ 哪儿

18. 我学习游泳 _____ 了。

Ⓐ 三月　　　　Ⓑ 星期三　　　Ⓒ 三个星期

19. 中国很 _____，中国人也很 _____。

Ⓐ 多　　　　　Ⓑ 大　　　　　Ⓒ 少

20. 你觉得这儿的天气 _____？

Ⓐ 怎么　　　　Ⓑ 什么　　　　Ⓒ 怎么样

读对话，选择正确的答案。
Write down the letter next to the phrase that best completes the sentence.

> **例** EXAMPLE
> 小米：请坐！
> 朗朗：___C___。
> Ⓐ 对不起　Ⓑ 没关系　Ⓒ 谢谢

21. 朗朗：我可以和你一起玩电脑吗？

　　小米：_____，这不是我的电脑，这是我哥哥的。

　　Ⓐ 对不起　　　Ⓑ 没关系　　　Ⓒ 谢谢

22. 小米：朗朗，你会不会画画儿？

　　朗朗：_____。

　　Ⓐ 我会说汉语　　Ⓑ 我要去学校

　　Ⓒ 我不会画画儿

23. 朗朗：你的书包_____！

　　小米：谢谢！

　　Ⓐ 真好吃　　　Ⓑ 真高兴　　　Ⓒ 真漂亮

24. 朗朗：今天早上你去了哪儿？

小米：_____。

Ⓐ 我在看医生　　Ⓑ 我去了医院　　Ⓒ 头很疼

25. 小米：你早上几点_____？

朗朗：早上七点半。

Ⓐ 起床　　　　　Ⓑ 睡觉　　　　　Ⓒ 放假

26. 朗朗：你现在在弹钢琴吗？

小米：是的。

朗朗：你要弹多久？

小米：_____。

Ⓐ 七点四十分　　Ⓑ 四十分钟　　　Ⓒ 几点

27. 小米：这个西瓜多少钱？

朗朗：_____。

Ⓐ 八块　　　　　Ⓑ 两只　　　　　Ⓒ 绿色的

28. 朗朗：乖乖兔买杯子做什么？

小米：送给她爸爸，＿＿＿＿＿＿＿＿＿＿＿。

Ⓐ 她爸爸是医生　　　　　　Ⓑ 她爸爸爱吃面条

Ⓒ 她爸爸喜欢喝茶

29. 朗朗：贝贝猪现在怎么样？

小米：＿＿＿＿＿＿＿＿＿＿，他在睡觉。

Ⓐ 没有说话　　　Ⓑ 不要说话　　　Ⓒ 请说话

第 30~32 题

写出正确的序号组成句子。
Write down the letter of each phrase in the correct order as the sentences.

> **例 EXAMPLE**　❶ 去　❷ 多久　❸ 你　❹ 要
>
> ③ ④ ① ② ?

30. ❶ 去　　❷ 你要　　　地方　　❹ 几个

＿＿＿＿＿＿＿＿＿＿＿＿＿＿＿＿？

31. ❶ 你要　　❷ 放假了　　❸ 哪儿　　❹ 去

＿＿＿＿＿＿＿＿＿＿＿＿＿＿＿＿？

32. ❶ 熊猫　　❷ 一只　　❸ 动物园　　❹ 有

＿＿＿＿＿＿＿＿＿＿＿＿＿＿＿＿。

我要去中国

放假了我要去中国，
中国的地大人也多。
爸爸和妈妈一起带着我，
高高兴兴地走遍中国。
登长城，看鸟巢，
还有那上海的世博园。

须使用课程CD-ROM或在线课程（www.yes-chinese.com），跟着音乐演唱。
This lyric should be sung along with the music found in the course CD-ROM or in the online lessons.

单元四		Unit Four
怎样	怎么样	how
动物	动物	animals
园	动物园	zoo
熊	熊猫	panda
虎	老虎	tiger
外	外面	outside
下雨	下雨	raining
太阳	太阳	sun
热		hot
冷		cold
天气		weather
一起		together
没有		not

单元五		Unit Five
铅笔	铅笔	pencil
少	多少	how much
钱		money
块两	两块钱	two Yuan
东	东西	stuff
衣服	衣服	clothes
昨	昨天	yesterday
了		
杯	杯子	cup
送给	送给	send to
茶	喝茶	drink tea
弟	弟弟	younger brother
妹	妹妹	younger sister

单元六　Unit Six

早	早上	early morning
医	医生	doctor
院	医院	hospital
房间	房间	house
睡觉	睡觉	sleep
得	觉得	feel
疼		ache
晚	晚上	night
半	七点半	half past seven
分钟	分钟	minutes
北京	北京	Beijing
怎么		how

单元七　Unit Seven

床	起床	get up
午	下午	afternoon
弹钢琴	弹钢琴	play the piano
影	电影	movie
椅	椅子	chair
放假	放假	holiday
比		than
地方	地方	place
海	上海	Shanghai
久	多久	how long